About the Author

Maria Shaw is a professional astrologer, intuitive, and tarot expert. She is the astrologer for the *TV Guide Channel*. A regular contributor to various New Age publications, Maria also writes monthly astrology columns for *Soap Opera Digest, Tigerbeat,* and *BOP!* magazine. She is the author of *Maria Shaw's Star Gazer: Your Soul Searching, Dream Seeking Guide to the Future.*

To Write to the Author

If you wish to contact the author or would like more information about this book, please write to the author in care of Llewellyn Worldwide and we will forward your request. Both the author and publisher appreciate hearing from you and learning of your enjoyment of this book and how it has helped you. Llewellyn Worldwide cannot guarantee that every letter written to the author can be answered, but all will be forwarded. Please write to:

Maria Shaw
℅ Llewellyn Worldwide
P.O. Box 64383, Dept. 0-7387-0523-3
St. Paul, MN 55164-0383, U.S.A.

Please enclose a self-addressed stamped envelope for reply, or $1.00 to cover costs. If outside U.S.A., enclose international postal reply coupon.

Many of Llewellyn's authors have websites with additional information and resources. For more information, please visit our website at http://www.llewellyn.com

Maria Shaw's
Tarot
for Teens

Llewellyn Publications
St. Paul, Minnesota

First Edition
Second Printing, 2004

Book design and editing by Karin Simoneau
Cover design by Ellen Dahl
Image on book cover © 2004 by SuperStock, Inc.
Image on kit cover © 2004 by Thinkstock
Interior illustrations by Llewellyn Art Department

Tarot cards used in this book are from *Universal Tarot* © by A. E. Waite and R. De Angelis. Used with permission by the Italian publisher Lo Scarabeo.

Library of Congress Cataloging-in-Publication Data
Shaw, Maria, 1963–
　Maria Shaw's tarot kit for teens / Maria Shaw.
　　p.　cm.
　ISBN 0-7387-0523-3
　1. Tarot. I. Title: Tarot kit for teens. II. Title.

BF1879.T2S539 2004
133.3'2424—dc22　　　　　　　2004046511

Llewellyn Worldwide does not participate in, endorse, or have any authority or responsibility concerning private business transactions between our authors and the public.

All mail addressed to the author is forwarded but the publisher cannot, unless specifically instructed by the author, give out an address or phone number.

Any Internet references contained in this work are current at publication time, but the publisher cannot guarantee that a specific location will continue to be maintained. Please refer to the publisher's website for links to authors' websites and other sources.

Llewellyn Publications
A Division of Llewellyn Worldwide, Ltd.
P.O. Box 64383, Dept. 0-7387-0523-3
St. Paul, MN 55164-0383, U.S.A.
www.llewellyn.com

Printed in the United States of America

Dedicated to Patricia "Angie" Moore, for passing on the knowledge of the tarot to me years ago.

Other Books by Maria Shaw

Maria Shaw's Star Gazer

Forthcoming Book

Maria Shaw's Book of Love

Contents

Introduction

WELCOME, AND CONGRATULATIONS! You are about to embark on a phenomenal journey. Just as millions of people over hundreds of years have studied the tarot's secrets and symbols, you too will experience the magic of this ancient art. Use these cards to help you increase spiritual awareness, tune into your intuitive side, and predict the future! You don't need to know anything about the tarot. You won't even have to memorize the card meanings. All you need is a tarot deck and a willingness to learn. So c'mon. Think of a question or two you're dying to ask, draw a card from your new deck, and then look up its meaning. You'll have an answer in no time! Not to mention, a whole lot more insight.

Here's What You'll Learn

The meanings of the cards: We'll explore in-depth the descriptions and interpretations of each card in your deck. Find out the card's positive and negative qualities. Every card has a story to tell. You'll get keywords and catchy phrases to help you memorize each one, if you so desire.

How to give readings: You'll be a pro in no time! Reading the tarot is not difficult. With my easy-to-follow layouts and formats, you'll discover favorite spreads. You can even design your own. To make your readings extra special and increase their accuracy, learn a few insider tips and secrets that professionals use.

Greater insight into your future and that of others: Everyone is interested in his or her future. It's human nature to be curious about what lies ahead. You'll find yourself very popular among your friends as you make amazing predictions for them. Plus you'll be developing communication and counseling skills.

Words of Tarot Wisdom from Maria

There's a definite science to reading the tarot. The art is in the interpretation.

How you interpret the cards is just as important as knowing the layouts and meanings of the symbols. You will develop your own special way of working with a deck.

Follow your hunches. Use the cards to help others by giving them hope. Even if you see something negative, you have a responsibility to warn your friends about what may be coming, because they then have the opportunity to make changes to avoid conflicts and hurt. Everyone has the power of free will to create his or her own destiny and reality.

To read the tarot is to take on great responsibility. You must always read ethically and honestly. If you use the tarot for negative purposes or as a form of manipulation to influence someone or merely to benefit yourself, it will stop working with you and your readings may prove to be inaccurate at some point. The spiritual power of the cards will begin to fade. When you use the tarot sincerely and for your higher good to assist others, it can always be a trusted guide.

Maria's First Lessons and Observations

I was adopted, and I didn't meet my birth mother, Angie, until I was twenty-two. We met when her sister (my aunt) arranged for us to meet at Angie's apartment, which was in a suburb of Detroit. I was very excited to spend time with her and to get to know her better. She was a real-estate agent by day and an astrologer by night.

I can objectively and honestly say that my mother was the best tarot reader I ever knew; she was almost 100 percent accurate. She died of cancer in her early fifties (and yes, she knew she would die young). Years before she died, she did an astrology reading for herself. Even though her chart showed she might pass on during middle age, she continued to be a chain smoker up until her dying days.

My mother passed down her knowledge and love of the tarot to me. It has always been my wish to pass her information on to others. I feel the best gift you can give someone, besides your attention and time, is the gift of knowledge. If a person can help others to expand their own intuition and learn something valuable, then he or she is doing a great service. Knowledge is power, and by sharing knowledge, we can all gain. Teaching is also a gift. I know there are millions of young people out there in the world who are searching for answers, for a higher truth. Know that this truth is within you. You possess all of the truth and wisdom of the world, but you need to learn how to unlock this knowledge and let it flow. We're all born with a higher self. Getting in touch with that higher self connects us to the Light, and in turn, we can help others spread goodness and love throughout the world. That's why we're all here anyway: to serve and love others.

My mother had read my cards and told me about some negative things that could possibly happen to me. Sometimes it's difficult to read for people with whom you are close. You don't want to see bad things or tell them anything that would hurt or worry them. But my mom was always honest. She said, "You know I will always tell you the truth. Whatever I see, I'll let you know." I respected that about my mother. She had a way with people. She always found the positive in every situation, no matter how difficult or challenging the circumstance. She could find a bright light amid the darkness.

I still remember very clearly the first time she taught me to read the tarot. I was excited, but at the same time the entire process seemed so overwhelming. I always looked at my mother's cards as if they held some magical power. All of the answers to any of the questions I would ever seek were in those cards. Her cards were worn and stained, but she always kept them in a wooden box when she wasn't using them. The box was kept next to her tarot books, which I later came to inherit. My first lesson began after my mother lit a candle and told me to shuffle the cards, fan them out on the dining room table, and pick thirteen of them. She said the most important thing was to concentrate on the cards I chose. I then had to run my hand over the deck and feel the energy vibrating from it. If I was drawn to a certain card, I was to pick it up and place it facedown in a pile. I drew my cards with much anticipation. My mother then instructed me to lay the cards out facedown in two neat rows. Then I flipped the first card over and read it, and so on. In the beginning of my earliest tarot lessons, I will admit, there were times I didn't see a darn thing. I would concentrate, but nothing would come. My mom said I was concentrating too hard. "Look at the picture on each card," she instructed, and then she asked me, "What do you feel? What does that card mean to you?" I began to turn my statements into questions. For instance, if she seemed to be upset about something, instead of saying, "It seems like you're upset," I would ask, "Are you feeling upset about something?" She confirmed or acknowledged each question for me.

As time went on, I continued to read for her. Then she threw me into the lion's den. She had her friends (all psychics and tarot readers) over one night and I was to give them all individual readings. It wasn't that bad because they knew me a little bit and went easy on me. But as time went on, my predictions for these professionals started coming true, and they began asking me for opinions on personal things. I remember one of my mother's friends who was an excellent psychic. She phoned to ask me what type of condo she should buy. I consulted my own deck of cards and it said she should purchase a two-bedroom, two-bathroom condo, painted yellow. I questioned my prediction. Why would a single woman need two bedrooms and two baths? A few days later she told my mother that that's exactly what she made an offer on! I was on my way! My aunt started scheduling house parties for me. I was really working hard, using my psychic abilities and the cards at the same time. One party led to more referrals, and then more people called to book me. Word-of-mouth advertising was great!

I started doing the big expos in large cities. I rented a table at the larger psychic fairs and was charging ten dollars for a ten-minute reading. Some days I was doing up to forty readings in an eight-hour period. Boy, was I tired, but I was loving the opportunity to help give insight to so many people. My first big expo was in Detroit, and at one point a young blonde woman came to sit down at my table. "Can you give me a reading?" she asked.

"Sure!" I answered. I was so nervous. All of the seasoned veterans had their tables set up so beautifully, with elaborate table coverings, signs, and artwork. I had a card table with no cloth and one dream catcher hanging off the corner of it. My first client of the day shuffled the deck and drew some cards. My mind went blank because I was so nervous, then I took a deep breath and asked her what she wanted to concentrate on. She said she needed to know about her marriage and love life. The cards she drew didn't look good, as they indicated marital problems. She told me that she was indeed getting a divorce, and that she was very unhappy. That's when I realized I couldn't leave this girl hanging; actually, after that experience I knew I could never finish a reading without looking forward into a person's life to see where hope and joy lay—a final outcome, if you will. I believe everything happens for a reason. Even those circumstances that are not favorable at the time will result in something positive. There can't be rainbows without rain.

Sometimes we need to go through a challenging period to get to a better place. So I told this young woman that she was likely going to go through with the divorce and that her soon-to-be ex-husband would draw battle lines. But I also looked further to see what this drastic change in her life would bring. I saw another marriage a few years down the road, more children, and a happy life. She felt better. She confirmed many things I had told her, and left with hope, knowing things would be all right. Years later, she contacted me and shared great news; all that I had told her would happen, did happen. She was remarried and so glad she left her former abusive husband. I remembered her because her reading was my first at a big expo. But I also remember her because that reading changed the way I read. Our job is to show people the good and the not so good, but also to give them hope.

I don't mean you should lie to your clients, but, with honesty, look further into the cards and see what lies ahead.

Keep going past all of the challenges you see until you reach an end result, a lesson, and a reward. As a tarot reader, your cards are the flashlight as your clients walk a darkened path. They may not see any hope or light. You can light their way. Give them a different way of looking at things, a new perspective, but remember, it is they who choose to walk the path.

I used to worry obsessively about my clients. After reading I couldn't shake the faces of all those who came to me with problems and concerns. Likewise, there were many happy people who were anxious to know where the future might lead them. But it was the ones who had the most hardships that had the biggest impact on me, and I found it hard to stop thinking, caring, and worrying about them. The most I could do was pray for them, and I did.

Sometimes I did not like the things I saw and I questioned my judgment. Can I really tell this person that? Should I even go there? As time went on, I learned to trust my first thoughts and impressions, and this never served me wrong. You would be amazed at how much information we get, and how much information the clients give us. They share with us some of the most personal and intimate details of their lives and relationships. Some of the information makes me blush. I learn of long-guarded family secrets and plots against others, longings for distant loves as well as fears and sorrows. I am looked on as a close confidant and friend. Some people become too dependent on me and I have to distance myself from them so they can make their own decisions. That is one of the problems with reading for someone who is going through a crisis. They can become emotionally dependent on you. That's not healthy for them. They need to stand on their own two feet. Be supportive, but don't make decisions for them.

There is no better feeling than helping someone celebrate a happy moment. I love to give readings to clients who are drawing great cards filled with messages of joy and fortune. You should see their eyes light up as you tell them the good news coming. To be the bearer of such wonderful news makes one very popular indeed!

Yet, reading the tarot is a great responsibility. It shouldn't be taken lightly. For true professionals, it's not a job, but a calling. Sure there are scam artists and charlatans out there, giving true tarot professionals a bad rap, but for those committed to the craft, reading becomes a way of life.

It's a very spiritual way of life, I might add. Dealing with the messages of the tarot day after day, you will start to look at things from a higher perspective, and that's probably the greatest gift I have received from my experience with the tarot. Your motivation becomes selfless. What can I learn from this? What is the most spiritual way to do something? How can I help? Spirituality becomes an everyday part of your existence.

Whatever you choose to do with the knowledge you glean from this book, whether you use it to help your friends, increase your own intuition, or are considering using the tarot in a larger way like I have, know that it can and will change your life. I have come so far from that very first night in my mom's apartment. I've inherited many things from her since she's passed on, but the greatest gift she gave me is this spiritual tool we call the tarot. She's passed on knowledge that can never be taken away from me. It's something that's been around for many centuries, and will continue to thrive. Now I'd like to pass this gift on to you.

The History of the Tarot

THE ANCIENT ART OF TAROT reading has been enjoyed for centuries all over the world. There are many different accounts of where and when the tarot originated. Respected researchers say the tarot first appeared in northern Italy between 1420 and 1440.

However, it is in Ferrara, Italy, that we can trace actual documentation of the tarot back to 1422. The oldest decks, which are still in existence today, date back to 1450 and are on display in Milan and Ferrara.

The earliest cards were lavishly designed and hand-painted. They depicted the nobles—kings and queens and their courts. These cards were modeled after a regular deck of playing cards, unlike the sets we see today.

The tarot may have developed fifty years after the playing cards from Islam were introduced in Europe. It is said playing cards found their way into European cities around 1375 and were adapted from the Islamic Mamluck cards. These decks had suits of Cups, Swords, Coins, and Sticks, as well as court cards that included a King and two male counterparts.

Tarot designers used this system, but added the Fool, Trumps, and Queens.

Surprisingly, written documents show that the tarot was not originally used for divination, but rather to play a card game, similar to bridge. Researchers claim that the tarot wasn't even connected to magic and the occult until more than a hundred years after its conception.

A 1589 trial in Venice may connect the deck with witchcraft, but I found no evidence that the tarot was used to give readings until the eighteenth century. Rather, it was used to compose poems that described characteristics and personalities, mainly of royalty. However, there are records that prove certain divination meanings were assigned to the tarot cards in the 1700s.

It's likely that the Italian Renaissance period helped the popularity of the tarot expand. More and more people consulted card readers for their insight, and after the 1780s the tarot became a recognized part of the occult. The earliest names of the deck can be traced back to Italy too. The cards were originally called *carte da trionfi,* meaning "cards of the triumps." Around the mid-1500s, the word *tarocco* was used to distinguish the cards from another card game called trumps. The French conjured up the word *tarot,* which we use today.

Fast forward a few hundred years, and a new tarot deck was born. The Waite-Smith deck was published in 1909. A. E. Waite, a member of the Hermetic Order of the Golden Dawn, created this deck, which is one of the most widely used and popular today. The artist was Pamela Colman Smith, and her illustrations used new symbolism of the time.

For years, the Waite-Smith deck was the only deck widely available in the United States, so many tarot fans and readers became very familiar with it.

Down through the centuries, the tarot has undergone many facelifts and artistic changes. But its message remains the same: By tuning into the vibration of the cards' images, we gain a deeper understanding of ourselves, our life path, and our future. There's ancient wisdom alive in these cards. They combine belief systems from the Hebrew Cabala, astrology, and numerology.

The Major and Minor Arcana

THERE ARE SEVENTY-EIGHT CARDS in the tarot deck, and these cards are divided into two units. Twenty-two are major arcana cards, and fifty-six are minor arcana. Arcana means "profound secrets."

The major arcana is connected to the big events in our lives, such as graduation, marriage, death, and any life-altering triumphs and tragedies. These are the most powerful cards in your deck because they represent life's "major" turning points, and as a result, their impact is more profound than that of all the other cards. When giving a reading, make special note of the major arcana because they will have the biggest effect on the overall picture of what lies ahead. The major arcana begins with the Fool, numbered zero. Some decks place the Fool first in the deck, and in others you will find that it is the last card in the major arcana.

The minor arcana is made up of the rest of the cards, and has to do with our day to day activities and issues such as work, school, and the like. These cards are divided into four suits: Wands, Cups, Swords, and Pentacles. Each card in the suit is numbered one to ten. These are followed by the four court cards: Page, Knight, Queen, and King. By tuning into the minor arcana's images, we can capture a glimpse into our everyday lives and the details that help make up the overall picture.

The Major Arcana

Remember, the major arcana cards are the most important and meaningful part of your deck. These are picture cards with a name or title at the bottom of each card. The major arcana is broken down into three groups consisting of seven cards each:

The material world: The first group deals with the outside world and situations connected to it. Think of your relationships, family, the laws of society, schooling, and the like. This group also includes possessions, the comforts of life, and the choices you make that determine how you live. The cards in this group include the Fool, the High Priestess, the Empress, the Emperor, the Hierophant, the Lovers, and the Chariot.

Intuitive nature: The second group of the major arcana concerns itself with your intuitive mind. It represents faith, hope, love, and spirituality. This grouping relates to decisions you make based on feelings rather than logic. For me, these cards concern themselves with issues that touch the heart. The cards in this group include Justice, the Hermit, the Wheel of Fortune, Strength, the Hanged Man, Death, and Temperance.

Change: The third group contains the most powerful cards in the entire deck. They combine the issues of the first two groups and will help or challenge your personal concerns and life path. These cards reach beyond society's rules and regulations, for they represent spiritual laws. In this set of seven, the power of the universe, which creates life-altering events and situations, is the most evident. The cards in this group include the Devil, the Tower, the Star, the Moon, the Sun, Judgment, and the World.

The Minor Arcana

The minor arcana is broken down into four separate suits of fourteen cards each. Forty of the minor arcana cards are like a regular deck of playing cards. The four other cards in each suit are called court cards. Each suit deals with a specific area of life. You could do a reading with just the major arcana, but it would be incomplete. The minor arcana reveal important details, such as people you will come in contact with, specific events, and so much more.

The Suits

Cups = love and relationships: Whenever you draw a Cups card, you will be dealing with love and affairs of the heart. This suit is also associated with spirituality and intuitive abilities. When you read this card, allow your intuition to guide you and let your feelings flow. Think emotions, intent, and desire. If you draw many cards in the Cups suit, recognize that situations and upcoming events will tend to be based on feelings rather than intellect.

Wands = actions, ambitions, activities: When you draw a Wand, recognize that this suit has to do with immediate actions taken. It represents a flurry of activity and energy.

Wands also represent people or situations that are exciting and creative. Wands stand for growth and development. So if you see a lot of this specific suit in your reading, know that a situation or an idea is in the beginning stages of development and ripe for expansion.

Pentacles = money, home and family, career, security: Pentacles are goldlike discs. When you draw a Pentacle card, anything that represents security may be an issue. For some people this suit relates entirely to money, but for others, the Pentacles represent "a sense of belonging." Think family, church, friendship circles, and work. This suit can also represent results of actions taken and, oftentimes, prosperity and payoffs.

Swords = conflicts, problems: The suit of Swords generally represents arguments, strife, commotion, and conflicts of all sorts. But not just physical conflict. It can represent moral and ethical concerns too. These cards link themselves to any situation or crisis that creates turmoil. If many swords come up in a reading, there could be several challenges or difficulties to go through before one can reach a goal and move past problems.

Court Cards

Notice that the minor arcana cards are numbered one to ten. In addition, there are four court cards in each suit: Page, Knight, Queen, and King. Let's discover what these "royal" cards mean.

Page: Represents a young person, children, students, and communications of all sorts, such as e-mails, phone calls, and letters. In medieval times, pages were young men and boys who worked for kings, queens, and royal courts. They waited on their lords and ladies hand and foot. Oftentimes, they were used to deliver messages and town notices. Many a youngster wanted to be a page, for it was the education they needed to assure them a good position when they grew up. Their ultimate goal was to become a knight. In the tarot, a Page doesn't always represent a male figure. Such a card may also refer to a girl or young woman.

Knight: Represents people who take action and are goal setters. Sometimes related to challenges, life's responsibilities, and self-discovery. Hundreds of years ago, knights were men that served the king and his court. They were very well respected. It was an honor to be a knight. These men had a variety of duties, such as discovering new lands and territories as well as competing in contests that tested their skills and abilities. In your deck, Knights represent men and women who take up quests. They are goal-oriented and high achievers.

Queen: Feminine power. In the tarot, Queens represent emotions, the important women in your life, home, family, and intuition. The Queen is not a ruler like the King. Her role is that of a positive partner to his majesty. Yet, she is also considered a strong symbol of feminine power. Young married women, mothers, and even older matronly ladies are associated with the Queen card. However, in a few instances, this card can represent a man if he has maternal, emotional, and caring qualities.

King: Powerful men or men in positions of authority. Masculine energy. Decision-making. The King is the symbol of masculine power in the tarot. Usually, Kings represent men. However, women who exert much power and authority in the outside world can also be considered Kings. Since his majesty was the ruler of his land and people, his primary duty was to preserve the well-being of his kingdom. King qualities include self-assertion and leadership abilities.

Number Cards

Every card in your tarot deck, except for the court cards, is linked to a certain number. Based on numerology principles, each number has a unique meaning. Let's look further, but first I'd like to highlight a few very important cards.

Aces: Aces are the most potent card in any suit. They are number one! They offer help in difficult situations. The ace is mostly positive. When you draw one, you will usually find that help or luck is on its way.

Eights: Eights are special because they represent infinity. If you draw an eight anywhere in your spread, take extra notice because eights represent major changes that may come about in your life.

The Fool: The Fool's number is zero, and it doesn't fit in any of the arcana's three sections mentioned earlier. Therefore, it doesn't have as much strength and power as the major arcana cards. However, it is considered more potent than the minor arcana. Some readers place the Fool at the beginning of the major arcana group, and others put it at the end. Both ways are fine, but I prefer to place it at the beginning. The Fool represents a new adventure, and every time I do a reading, I look at the session as an "adventure" to unlock some exciting news and information. When you draw the Fool, think of yourself as ready to embark on a new adventure. Know that change is inevitable.

Individual Numbers

Now let's look at some key words to consider regarding individual numbers.

Aces: Luck, new beginnings. A plan, situation, or condition is about to take off. Something is in the beginning stages of development. It could be positive or negative depending on the position of the card.

Twos: Commitments and choices. Two represents a stagnant or waiting period. Expect more to be revealed as time progresses. Twos mean a reunion or a coming together. Sometimes a surprise of some sort is revealed.

Threes: Plans, communication. Friends, group activities, new places, and new faces are all related to the number three. Threes will, sometimes, suggest delay. But not to worry, they usually indicate that future achievements will come to pass.

Fours: Creation, action. Fours mean that something is happening. They represent the manifestation of an idea or a foundation on which something new can be built.

Fives: Challenges, problems. Expect changes, either lucky or unlucky. If you are greeted with many five cards, try to keep a balance in your life.

Six: Happiness, contentment. You can overcome many obstacles with the help of a six. Sixes bring adjustments and opportunities to create more harmony.

Sevens: Options, choices. Through experiences, the sevens will help you gain much wisdom and understanding. Sometimes this number represents a period of solitude. Unexpected opportunities could present themselves as well.

Eights: Experience, commitment. Eights mean you will be able to accomplish what you set out to do. Eights are usually beneficial, even if they fall in a challenging or negative position.

Nines: Working it out, contentment. Nine means completion, the final stage to something, or fulfillment.

Tens: Resistance, caution. You may have to come to terms with issues from the past that you had hoped to avoid. The past may come back to help or haunt you. In some circumstances, you may be asked to exert more caution than usual.

(Note: If there is an abundance of one suit in your overall reading, the main theme of the reading may very well jump out at you. Say you have a lot of Cups; you can expect much news about love and relationships. If there are several Pentacles, know that security or money will be the main theme.)

Now that we've covered the basics of the tarot, let's examine some other principles before we get into the layout and interpretation chapters.

These next two chapters are just as important to a good reading as knowing the meaning of the cards.

Tarot Tips

WHAT KIND OF CARDS should you get? Because this book comes with a deck, you're covered. If you are interested in purchasing another deck, however, there are possibly hundreds of different types of tarot cards on the market today. How do you choose? I suggest you go to a bookstore or a New Age boutique that offers a good selection. Then pick through the cards that you are most drawn to.

What appeals to you? If there are sample decks that are already open, look through them. Ask if you can open a deck you are particularly interested in. Feel how the deck fits in your hand. Fan the cards out. What feelings do you get from them? Do you feel good about the cards? Shuffle them. Do you still feel drawn to them. If the answer is yes, this is the right deck for you!

Card Care

Your cards represent sacred symbols. It's important to keep this in mind and respect the tarot as an ancient art form. I always tell my clients not to use the tarot as if it were a game or a toy. Yes, your deck can provide you with hours of fun and enlightenment, but it needs to be taken seriously too. For in it, there is a wealth of information at your fingertips.

Don't let anyone play with your cards. You should be the only person to work with them and read them. Your friends will undoubtedly be shuffling and touching the deck, but it's important that your energy is the primary energy intertwined with the cards. Anyone else's energy could lessen or dampen the accuracy the deck will have when you read from it. So after you give your buddies a reading it's a good idea to "cleanse" the cards of your friend's energy. You can do this very simply by imagining a bright white light around your deck, by running your hand over the fanned out cards very slowly, or by holding the entire deck between the palms of your hands and sending positive, cleansing energy through them.

Sometimes the cards will retain impressions and energy of people who touch or use them. Therefore, you want to keep your cards free of any "vibrations" so they are "clean" every time you read them. When you're not using the cards, wrap them in silk, cotton, or a natural fabric, as impressions and energy don't cling to these fabrics. You can use a silk scarf or purchase a square piece of fabric at a fabric store. Also, many people store their wrapped cards in a decorative wooden box.

Make Your Own Tarot Bag

Because this book is part of a kit, your cards have their very own bag. If, however, you would like to create your own card sleeve or bag to put your deck in, this section is for you! And for those who would like to personalize the bag in their kit, read the last paragraph. It'll give you some cool decorating ideas to embellish it. Are you artistic? Creative? Then you'll probably come up with all sorts of ideas to personalize it as well.

Even if you've never sewn a button on a shirt, the simple instructions that follow will show you in a few easy steps how to create a special bag for your cards.

The important thing to remember is to pick the right type of fabric (again, use silk, cotton, or a natural fabric). Once you have the fabric, personalize it by embroidering, painting, or drawing designs on it. I have seen elaborate designs consisting of suns, moons, and stars that were painted on the bags. Some artists choose to draw their initials on the front. Others add tassels and fringe. The cost can be very inexpensive, depending on what type of fabric and designs you choose.

You will need the following:

· Needle and thread

· A piece of fabric

· A piece of decorative string or rope to use as a tie

Step 1: The average-size cards run about 2½ inches by 4 inches, so you'll want to get a piece of fabric that measures 6 by 9 or larger, depending on the size of your specific cards. Measure your deck and allow for at least one extra inch on all sides to hold the deck comfortably.

Step 2: Make a ½-inch fold along the two six-inch sides of the material, and sew each fold, leaving an opening on both sides (as you will pull the string through these openings). Fold the fabric in half, right sides together, matching the two seams you just sewed at the top.

Step 3: Using a ¼-inch seam, sew the wrong sides of the nine-inch fold of the fabric, making sure not to sew over the openings at the top.

Step 4: Turn the fabric right side out, thread the string through the openings (attach a safety pin to one end of the string, then guide the string through the openings), and decorate the outside as you wish.

That's all there is to it. Now, slip your cards in. Use the rope/string to wrap around the bag and tie in a pretty bow. You now have a custom-designed card sleeve (tarot bag).

Here are a few ideas for decorating the outside of your bag:

- Glue rhinestones and sequins to the fabric for extra sparkle
- Sew or iron on a patch of the sun or moon
- Glue or sew different colored feathers on the bottom of the bag so they dangle
- With a permanent marker, write your name or initials on the front of the bag
- With a glitter pen or colored marker, draw stars all over the bag
- Add fringe
- Hot glue crystal chips in rose quartz, amethyst, or your favorite semi-precious gems to the outside
- Add a simple needlepoint design
- Paint a star/sun/moon motif

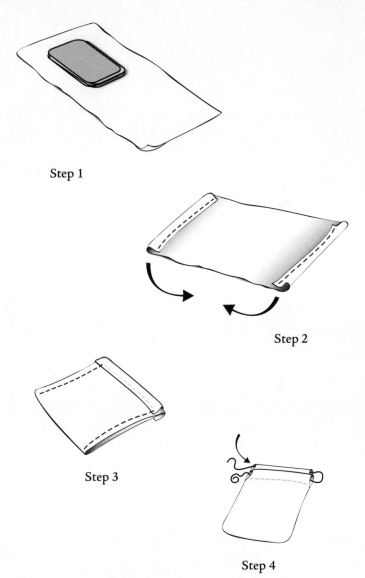

Step 1

Step 2

Step 3

Step 4

Instructions for Making Your Tarot Bag

Preparing for a Reading

BEFORE GIVING A READING, you'll want to create the right mood. Some people light candles or burn incense. You can play soothing instrumental music to create a relaxed atmosphere. Others prefer to meditate or pray. Before beginning a reading, I envision a beautiful white light that surrounds me and the person I'm reading for. The white light is a light of protection and peace. Your mind should be clear and relaxed. Never give a reading if you're upset, angry, tired, or in a bad mood.

If you choose to light candles or burn incense, make sure you get your parent's permission. And use caution, as some people are allergic to the smell of certain incenses. Also, never leave a candle unattended. Always blow it out when you've finished your reading or if you need to leave the room. We wouldn't want the house to burn down!

I feel it is always nice to start with a short prayer. You could ask the universe, your angels, or spirit guides for help in receiving messages. A prayer or affirmation could go something like this:

> I am open to receiving the messages the universe wishes to bring me. Please allow spiritual wisdom

and truths to filter through me for my highest good, and that of (friend's name, if applicable). Amen.

When you are giving a friend a reading, it is very important that you do not share or pass on any personal information (secrets) your "client" has shared with you during the session. The same goes for the messages you get from the cards, unless, of course, your client gives you permission. It would be unethical to gossip or tell other people what showed up in the reading. A tarot reader's job is similar to that of a priest. Confidentiality is a must!

The information between you and your client should always be kept private.

How to Cut the Cards

Are you ready? There are many different techniques you can use to begin a reading. The most common way to start is to shuffle the cards. Then cut the deck with your left hand into three piles. Pick up the piles, put them together, and fan the cards out on a table.

Some tarot readers fan all of the cards out (facedown) and mix them up. Then they'll choose cards they feel drawn to. Other readers shuffle them like an ordinary deck of playing cards and fan them out. A client then chooses several cards he or she is drawn to. Some people just take the cards, one by one, from the top of the deck and lay them out. All of these ways are fine. One is no better than the other. It's a matter of personal preference, but choosing the cards you want to read is important.

Take great care and don't hurry when selecting cards. Run your hand over the fanned-out cards. Which cards draw energy to you? Which are calling you? These are the cards you should choose. Pick them up with your left hand if you are right handed. If you're left handed, use your right. This is a magic moment. Choosing your cards is like a ritual. If you honor the process, your reading will be accurate and the tarot will honor you.

Think of your tarot deck as a friend who gives good advice. However, the advice that you receive is not written in stone. You can always change things because you have the power of free will. The tarot doesn't control your fate or destiny. It merely points out what could happen, reveals your subconscious thoughts, and aids in giving you ideas and a clearer picture into the future.

A Beginner's Layout

There are dozens of different card layouts you can do. A layout is also called a spread. You can even develop your own personalized spreads if you'd like. We'll discuss that a little later. But for now, you should start with a shorter spread and work your way up to the larger ones as you become acquainted and comfortable with the cards. The layouts in this book are easy to use, and there are even some that I designed especially for you, but I suggest you start with the following spread first. It's quick and easy. Once you understand this technique, move on to the others in this book.

Yes/No Reading

The simplest way to get an answer using the cards is to ask a yes or no question. As you shuffle the cards, think of your question over and over in your mind.

Ask it out loud if you wish. Fan the cards out and pick one that you are drawn to. If a card drops out of the deck while you're shuffling, you should read that one.

Ask a question that can be answered simply. Don't ask one that requires a detailed answer. Those questions can be saved for a longer layout. Phrase your question like this:

· Will I be dating someone this year?

· Will I pass my science test?

· Will I make a new best friend?

This reading won't give you specific times, so you won't know when things are likely to happen. It will only supply you with a yes or no answer. If you don't like the answer, don't ask the same question over and over, and don't ask the question twice in a twenty-four hour period. Accept your answer and decide which steps are best to take.

After you have drawn a card, go to chapter 9 and look up its meaning.

You can easily determine if the card is favorable or not. For example, if you were to ask the tarot, "Will I be dating soon?" and you drew the Lovers card, the obvious answer would be "yes." A new relationship is coming! Here's an even faster way to get an answer: shuffle the cards while concentrating on your question (without fanning the cards out), pull the card from the top of the deck, and look up its meaning in the book. Any way you feel comfortable is the "right" way. There is no wrong way to shuffle or pick cards. What's important is that you concentrate on the card that you are drawn to or feels right for you to choose. Some people don't even shuffle. They just pick up a card and see what its message is.

Create a Learner's Deck

One idea I'd like to share for those just learning the meaning of the cards is to purchase two decks. All come with a small instruction booklet containing the meanings of each individual card. Some sets come with a larger book, which includes pictures of the cards and their descriptions. I suggest that you use one set as a "learner's deck." Write the upright position meaning on the top of the corresponding card, and the reversed position on the bottom.

Then, as you practice, you won't have to look up the meanings each time in your booklet. You'll memorize each card easily this way and eventually won't need the learner's deck. The upright position is when the card is drawn upright, and the reversed position means the card is drawn upside down.

Asking Questions

Be specific when you ask a question of the tarot. If you don't understand the answer that the tarot is giving you, ask for clarification by choosing another card immediately.

Only ask one question at a time. Go with what the tarot is telling you. Don't second guess or dismiss an answer, but know that you can change the outcome of anything that is presented because you have the power of free will. The tarot is not the last word. You are in complete control of your life and destiny. The tarot is only a tool and a guide. But with its help you can unlock subconscious feelings and even confirm what you already know in your heart to be true.

Another good rule of thumb is not to confuse the tarot by asking too many combined questions. For example, I wouldn't phrase a question like this: "Who will I meet, and when, and what will he look like?"

Break your questions down into three separate ones, and ask them individually, as such:

1. "Who will I meet?"

2. "When will we meet?"

3. "What will he look like?"

If you ask questions one by one, the tarot is much more likely to give you specific details, and the cards are easier for you to interpret too!

Reading for Other People

You can do a reading for another person even if he or she is not present. You should first close your eyes and visualize the person you are reading for. Think of the person as you shuffle the cards, and then choose the cards that you feel drawn to. Sometimes it helps to have a photo of that person nearby, or even have him or her on the other end of the phone line!

If a reading is done in person, ask your client to be open-minded. And advise him or her not to tell you anything or reveal extra information unless you ask. For some readers, too much information influences the way they interpret the cards. It is perfectly fine, however, for your client to tell you what area he or she is most interested in learning about. You may even ask your client, "What do you hope to hear about? What is your primary focus now?"

Also, tell your clients to sit directly in front of you so you can "pick" up on their energy field. Tell them not to block the flow of energy between you two by crossing their arms or legs. Have them relax. You should choose where you wish to sit first; choose a spot where you feel comfortable and at ease. Make sure you leave ample time after you are finished reading the cards for any questions your clients may have. If they need clarification or more specific details on an issue or one particular card, it is fine to go back over it and even draw extra cards to reinforce and expand the information.

If you wish, ask your clients for feedback. Tell them to take a few weeks and see if any of your predictions have manifested, and to let you know how accurate the reading was. Many readers find that there are certain days of the month when the accuracy of their readings increases.

Good Days to Read

Just as everyone has good days and bad days, tarot readers can be "off" and "on" too, depending on their moods and energy levels. But did you know there are certain days in every month that are especially conducive for tapping into your "psychic energy"?

Information from the tarot seems to flow effortlessly on full moon days. It's especially exciting to give readings during the full moon because everyone is more sensitive and psychic at this time. You can consult a calendar to see when these days occur. The full moon is in effect three days before and three days after the specific day listed on calendars. Also, every two-and-a-half days the moon changes into a different zodiac sign. When the moon is in a water sign such as Cancer, Pisces, or Scorpio, people are also very sensitive and can tap into their intuition easily. Consult an astrology calendar, one that features the moon and its signs, for even more extra special days to give readings.

Why don't you test it out for yourself?

Dropped Cards

If a card drops out of the deck as you are shuffling or falls from it at any point, realize that this card may hold the answer you are seeking. You should definitely take notice of this particular card and read it first. Sometimes, this card is all you'll need to complete a reading. Other times it adds to or confirms what you are being told.

Timing Events

When reading the tarot, it is sometimes difficult to tell exactly when an event will happen. If you want to know the time of an event, it's important to phrase your question very specifically. You can also affirm that the reading you're doing is good for a day, a week, a month, or more. Before I begin a reading, I usually say out loud, "This reading is good for the next three months," or "This reading will give me information on what's transpiring this week." You may also choose a specific spread in this book designed with a certain timeframe in mind. Or you may just ask questions that are phrased as such: "Will I meet someone in the next week?"

Another point to keep in mind is that certain individual cards can help you pinpoint specific timeframes too. The major arcana usually represent things that are happening very soon, and the ace cards will tell you the season of the year in which you can expect things to happen. Just look at the picture on the card.

Ace of Wands = Autumn

Ace of Cups = Summer

Ace of Swords = Winter

Ace of Pentacles = Spring

The Court Cards

The King, Queen, and Page in any suit can also give you an idea of when something will happen. The Knight in any suit marks only the beginning or the end of an event. When he appears, expect a change immediately. Here's a look at time frames related to each court card. Interestingly enough, they correspond with the zodiac signs too. You will see the individual cards, the time frames that correspond to each, as well as the zodiac sign.

King of Wands: March 21–April 19 (Aries)

Queen of Wands: July 23–August 22 (Leo)

Page of Wands: November 22–December 21 (Sagittarius)

King of Cups: June 21–July 22 (Cancer)

Queen of Cups: October 23–November 21 (Scorpio)

Page of Cups: February 19–March 20 (Pisces)

King of Swords: September 23–October 22 (Libra)

Queen of Swords: August 23–September 22 (Virgo)

Page of Swords: April 20–May 20 (Taurus)

King of Pentacles: May 21–June 20 (Gemini)

Queen of Pentacles: January 20–February 19 (Aquarius)

Page of Pentacles: December 22–January 19 (Capricorn)

If you were to ask, "When will I get a new job?" and you draw the King of Wands, then the tarot is specifically telling you that a new position will come about between March 21 and April 19.

Besides timing events, the court cards can be used to describe people you will come into contact with. A King of Swords would be someone born between September 23 and October 22. In astrology, we know this person to be a Libra. If this Swords King appears in your spread, expect a Libra man or one with Libra-like qualities (fair, honest, easygoing) to appear in your life.

Ancient and Modern-Day Spreads

Thought for the Day: The Daily Theme Card

What will your day be like? This one card pick highlights the overall theme for the next twenty-four hours. When you get up each day, you can make the tarot a part of your morning routine. It's a good idea to have your cards handy so you don't forget to read them! Leave them on your night stand next to your alarm clock, or maybe even in the bathroom next to the toothpaste.

Here's what you should do:

Shuffle the cards and clear your mind. Breathe in and out in a slow, relaxed manner. Visualize a fluffy white cloud encircling your entire body. White stands for peace and protection. You will feel calm and relaxed as you visualize this white light all around you. Then when you feel you have shuffled the cards enough, spread them out on a table and pick one from the deck. Choose the card that you feel most drawn to, for it will have the most meaning. If you concentrate and take time to choose a card rather than rushing through the process, the card you draw will be the "right" one. Turn your card over and take a moment to examine your feelings as you look at it. How do you feel? Does the picture on the card make you feel anxious? Perhaps happy or excited? Do you feel sadness? Let the first impression that pops into your mind be a psychic guide. If you are experiencing a good feeling, know that this card's impression will set the tone for your entire day! You can carry that happy feeling with you all day long.

If the impression is one of sadness or negativity, take an extra moment or two to visualize something happy. If you felt lonely, visualize yourself surrounded by friends and family. If the card appears to suggest a "letdown" of some sort, you may say a positive affirmation out loud, such as, "I am able to overcome any difficulties this day may bring. I am happy, safe, and secure. Today will be a wonderful day!" Just the power of positive thinking can turn a potentially challenging day into a prosperous one.

Next, you will want to look up the card's definition in your tarot book and read it. It will apply to what you may experience throughout your day. For example, if the card is the Chariot, you can expect a short trip to come up at some point in the day. Or you may be planning a vacation. Your daily theme card can be left faceup on the top of your deck all day to remind you of what you should be expecting, doing, or preparing yourself for.

After all, it's good to be ready for anything that comes your way! If a card suggests that you use extra caution in your dealing with friends, it may help you to avoid an unnecessary argument. Forewarned is forearmed! Remember, you can change anything because you have the power of free will.

You could take a negative card and turn its vibration into a powerful and positive outcome. A positive card may tune you in to an opportunity that you would never have looked for if you hadn't drawn it. Making the tarot a part of your day can be enlightening, interesting, and revealing!

The Three-Card Spread

Another simple layout is the Three-Card Spread (or past, present, and future reading). Shuffle the deck, fan it out, and pick three cards. The first card you choose should be laid to your left. It represents your past, what has already happened, what you know to be true. The second card is to be placed directly in front of you. It deals with the current conditions around you. The third card is placed to the right and reveals what will happen in the near future as well as the outcome of an event or circumstance.

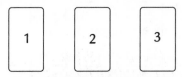

The Weekly Spread

It is best to do this reading (also called the Seven-Card Spread) on a Sunday, since most people begin their week first thing Monday morning. However, you may do it anytime. Shuffle the cards, choose one, and lay it at the top of the table. Turn it over and read it. Whatever the meaning, know that it is the main theme and influence for your entire week. For example, if you drew the Fool card, recognize that change and adventure may be the running theme. If you drew a card in the minor arcana's Cup suit, it is likely you will be dealing with love and relationships. You may also be quite emotional this week. Now pick seven more cards and lay them out across the table. Read the first card as "Monday" (or the first day following your reading), the second card as "Tuesday," the third as "Wednesday," and so on. Each card represents a day of the week and depicts what is likely to happen over the course of the next seven days. If your first card is a Pentacle and falls under Monday, consider it likely that money issues will come up.

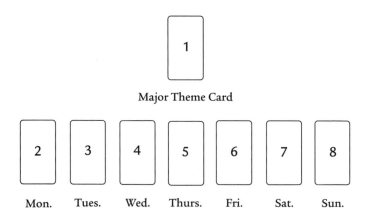

Major Theme Card

Mon.   Tues.   Wed.   Thurs.   Fri.   Sat.   Sun.

The Monthly Spread

The Monthly Spread is a layout of twenty-eight to thirty-one cards, depending on the number of days in the month in which you are conducting the reading. It is best done on the first day of the month or a few days before. You will find that this layout gives us a much more in-depth look at your life over the course of the next four weeks. It is likely to cover all areas of your life, including work, school, friends, travel, love, and so on. This reading may take an hour or so, depending on how well you understand and know the card meanings. So plan accordingly.

Take your time and don't rush through it. Keep a notepad handy to take notes as you interpret each card. You'll also find that the Monthly Spread will weave a story—a tale of what lies ahead—in greater detail than the shorter layouts you have come to learn.

Because there are so many cards to read, you may get stumped and not fully understand all of them until you complete the entire reading. Move on to another card if you don't "get it." It will make sense as you move through your reading at some point. Let's use the month of May for our example. There are thirty-one days in May, so you will shuffle your cards and draw thirty-one cards. Place them face down in five rows, with seven cards in each of the first four rows and three in the fifth row, as shown on the following page. Then, one at a time, turn the first card over and read it.

Now move to the second one. Flip over the third and write down your impressions, and so on. After you have completed the process with the thirty-one cards, look over your notes. Do you see a major theme? Are there more cards of one suit than another?

1	2	3	4	5	6	7
Day 1	Day 2	Day 3	Day 4	Day 5	Day 6	Day 7

8	9	10	11	12	13	14
Day 8	Day 9	Day 10	Day 11	Day 12	Day 13	Day 14

15	16	17	18	19	20	21
Day 15	Day 16	Day 17	Day 18	Day 19	Day 20	Day 21

22	23	24	25	26	27	28
Day 22	Day 23	Day 24	Day 25	Day 26	Day 27	Day 28

29	30	31
Day 29	Day 30	Day 31

Maria Shaw's Twelve-Month Spread

This layout is good for timing events. It's designed to provide an in-depth, longer reading that covers events likely to happen over the course of the year. You may prefer to do this one on New Year's Eve to see what the next twelve months hold in store for you. Or you may choose to do this spread on your birthday—that would be a great time too.

Shuffle the cards, fan them out, and pick twelve. The first card you draw should be the first one you read, and so on.

Place six cards in a row and six cards in another row beneath the first set, facedown. Turn the first card over. This card will tell you what is likely to happen during the current month of the reading. Turn to the page in this book that highlights this card, and read its meaning.

Now flip the second card over. It will tell you what to expect next month. The third card will give you insight on three months from now, and so on.

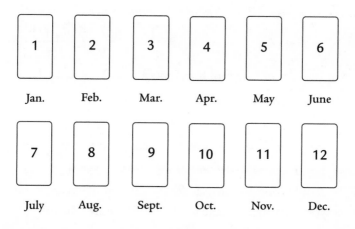

The Celtic Cross Spread

This is the spread that most professional tarot readers use and teach. It usually deals with one theme at a time. Lay the cards out following the order of sequence in the following diagram.

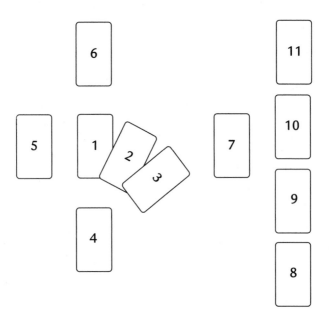

The position of each card highlights a specific issue.

1. Person (you or the person for whom you are reading).

2. Problems, concerns, possibilities. The card will offer solutions to a problem, advice to accomplish goals, or give warning of concerns or danger that may arise.

3. Resolutions. How to handle the concern. This card shows you what steps to take to achieve the desired outcome.

4. Past influences. This card tells you about a person or an event from the past that's affecting your current condition.

5. Current conditions. What's happening now. The mood or the atmosphere is represented by this card selection. It can be positive or negative.

6. Immediate or short-term future. This card predicts what is likely to happen over the next three months.

7. Present state of the issue/problem/concern. This card tells you exactly where the issue stands today and if it is negative or positive. It shows what stage the problem is at in relation to the final outcome.

8. Outside and other influences. People or circumstances that may determine, help, or hinder the desired outcome show up here.

9. Home. This card tells you about your home and foundation at the time of the reading.

10. Subconscious feelings, secrets, hidden things. Often, this card reveals how you are feeling about your concern or question.

11. Long-term future, final outcome. This card wraps up the entire reading. It shows you a final outcome and gives you a forecast for the next six months to one year.

Maria's Astrology Spread

My mother didn't teach me what the individual cards meant. That, I learned on my own. She taught me to use my psychic abilities when giving readings. Since she was an astrologer first and foremost, she taught me how to read the cards from an astrological perspective. This is the spread that I use most. Many times I will use my intuitive abilities as well as my astrological knowledge when I give a reading with this layout. I often teach my students to read tarot this way too. In some books I have seen this called the Zodiac Spread. I call it Maria's Astrology Spread, and lay thirteen cards out all the way across the table, as such.

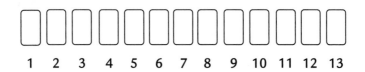

Each card represents a house in an astrology chart. There are twelve houses in a chart, each with a different theme or purpose. I also include a thirteenth card to "wrap up" the entire reading, to conclude it.

Card 1: Has to do with you. What is around you right now. The main concern or theme of the reading.

Card 2: Money, finances, material gain or loss.

Card 3: Siblings, travel, school, neighbors, communications of all sorts.

Card 4: Home and family, parents.

Card 5: Love affairs, kids, hobbies, luck, romance.

Card 6: Health, coworkers, pets.

Card 7: Committed relationships, partnerships, legal things.

Card 8: Money from others, debts you owe, psychic abilities, death.

Card 9: Higher education (college), grandparents, long-distance trips, legal issues, and foreign people, places, and things.

Card 10: Social standing, popularity, career.

Card 11: Friendships, group activities, goals, dreams.

Card 12: Hidden enemies, past lives, situations that involve hospitals, prisons, invalids, the past, karma.

Card 13: Wraps up the entire reading. The final outcome.

The Gypsy Spread

This is a popular layout handed down through the years by many fortunetellers. It has spanned many generations and is believed to have been first used by the traveling gypsies. Many readers use it today because it gives us an in-depth look at the past, present, and future. The Gypsy Spread has three rows of seven cards each. The first row relates to the past. Card one relates to the most distant past, and card seven the most recent.

The second row of seven cards is the present set, and will reveal to the reader exactly what is going on right now.

The last row of seven cards determines the future and what is likely to happen over the course of the next seven months.

(Note: Card number four in each row relates to the person for whom you are doing the reading and what he or she is most concerned about at the time.)

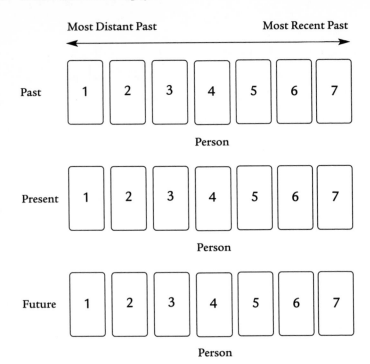

Love Layouts

Single and Searching

If your questions relate mainly to a new attraction or you're just curious about your love life, here's a layout designed especially for affairs of the heart!

The cards are laid out as such:

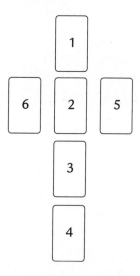

Card 1: You and what you are looking for in love. Your needs in a relationship.

Card 2: The object of your affection. If there's someone you're attracted to, this card represents that person. It will tell you what type of relationship or person may appear in your life or if there's an opportunity for love at this time.

Card 3: How strong and meaningful this relationship will be. How does your love interest feel about you?

Card 4: Tests and challenges the relationship may face. Obstacles in your path that could stop you from creating the type of relationship you desire. What could go wrong? Will it work out? Will the relationship be long lasting or just a quick crush?

Card 5: Where you are likely to meet this new crush, and possibly when you can expect love to enter your life.

Card 6: The final outcome of the relationship or your question regarding it. Will it last? Is it a good relationship? Will there be a breakup in the near future?

"I Think I'm In Love"

If you're already attached and want to know more about your current situation, here's the spread for you.

The cards are laid out as such:

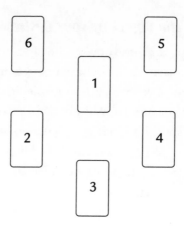

Card 1: You and your sweetie. How the relationship looks now.

Card 2: How the relationship looks as it progresses to the future. Will it be long lasting or a fast fizzle?

Card 3: How does he or she really feel about you? Is your sweetie head over heels in love, or is he or she fickle?

Card 4: Are there any issues or problems that could arise and cause you concern? Is there something you should be warned about and aware of in this relationship?

Card 5: What is the basis of this relationship? Physical attraction, friendship, or true love?

Card 6: What is the final outcome for the relationship? Will it lead to a deeper commitment, an eventual breakup, or die down to a mere friendship?

The Object of Your Desire

This is a reading for those of you who already are attracted to someone but a relationship hasn't gotten off the ground yet. It's for those of you who get butterflies in your stomach when you see someone. Do you wonder if he or she notices you too? This spread is blunt and to the point. If you can't handle rejection, don't proceed. But who knows? You may be pleasantly surprised with positive confirmation!

Shuffle the cards and divide them into five piles. Take the top card from each pile and lay it out as shown. One by one, read all five cards.

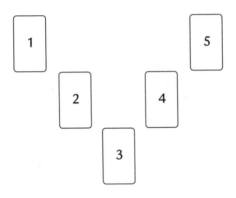

Card 1: Let's get right to the point. Does he or she even notice you? (If not, forget going any further until you attract attention.)

Card 2: Is there a chance for romance between you two?

Card 3: Is there anybody standing in the way of you two getting together? (An ex-girlfriend or old boyfriend? An overprotective parent?)

Card 4: Is this person really as cool as he or she appears to be? What is he or she really like?

Card 5: Now the big question! When can I expect to have a date with this guy or girl? (This will test what you remember about using the cards for timing.)

This layout is especially fun to do with friends. They've probably already asked your opinion on a certain crush. Now, you can consult your tarot and give your best buds some psychic insight!

The "Heart Breaker"

For those of you who have just been dumped and need to know why, there's hope out there.

Lay out as such:

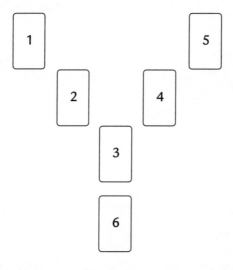

Card 1: What happened? The real reason behind the breakup and what you should know.

Card 2: Is there any chance of salvaging the relationship in the future. Can you get back together?

Card 3: How is he or she feeling now? Regretful? Relieved? Has he or she already moved on?

Card 4: Are there any new loves on the horizon? What type of new relationships can I expect?

Card 5: What was I to learn from this heartbreak?

Card 6: How long before I can move on and am able to love again?

Specialty Spreads

The "Big Question" Spread

When you desperately need a quick answer! If you have a concern or question that is very important and you need an immediate answer, "consult your tarot deck for deeper insight. The Big Question Spread is a four-card spread and it looks like this:

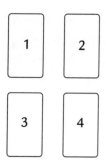

Card 1: The question, the problem, the concern; how it looks now.

Card 2: The obstacles standing in your path. What steps to take to achieve the desired result or goal.

Card 3: The opportunity that awaits you, and people that will help you. The reason this is happening. What are you learning about yourself?

Card 4: The final outcome.

The Guardian Angel/Spirit Guide Reading

I've designed this spread to help you get in touch with your angels and spirit guides. Your guides want to help you along your life path. They are always with you if you need them. Use this spread to connect with them. They want to share their powerful wisdom and be a part of your spiritual growth. You may receive direct information from them through your cards. This spread is designed to offer you knowledge in spiritual terms rather than focusing on mundane topics. Use this layout when you seek advice for moral, ethical, and spiritual concerns. But you may ask your angels and guides for guidance of any kind and at any time.

Shuffle your cards and pick seven (seven is a spiritual number). Lay them out as shown in the following diagram:

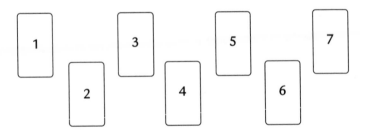

You will use your intuitive abilities more than ever now!

Close your eyes and ask your angels/spirit guides to be with you. Clear your mind and feel a sense of calmness and peace surrounding you. Ask out loud to receive messages from this higher source. Your request could go something like this:

> Dear Guardian Angel, I am calling upon you now to be near me. Please send me the messages you wish to reveal to me. Share your guidance and wisdom with me so that I am able to grow spiritually in my everyday life. Help me to interpret the messages of the tarot for my highest good and for the highest good of others.

Or you may also say:

> My Spirit Guide, Please be with me now and show me the way. Share with me your wisdom and knowledge so that I may use it for my highest good and for the highest good of others. As I read the tarot, be with me as my intuitive powers expand. May I feel the inner wisdom and gain the insight I need to help myself and my friends on their path.

Now place the seven cards in a circle, as shown on the following page.

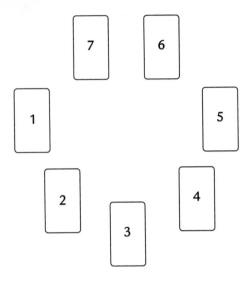

Card 1: Represents the main theme of your reading. What your angel or guide wishes to focus on in this reading.

Card 2: Who you can learn from. What type of person is coming into your life or is currently around who will offer guidance or assistance if you need it. (Remember, court cards are best at revealing this type of information.)

Card 3: The events or circumstances you will soon find yourself in.

Card 4: What you can learn from this experience.

Card 5: What steps to take to better your situation or experience more growth and happiness.

Card 6: The final outcome.

Card 7: Take a moment and look closely at this card. Now close your eyes but keep the card's image in your mind's eye. With eyes closed, ask your angel for an intuitive message. Go with the first message that pops into your mind.

Ask something like, "Are there any other messages you wish to send me right now?" Be open to any thoughts you feel, hear, or visualize. For some people, visualizing events comes easily. For others, thoughts pop into their heads. Still, there are many people who actually hear things. Be sure to thank your angel or spirit guide for their help and blessings.

Because you have just created a clear channel between you and your guide, it is quite possible you will receive messages for the rest of the day and perhaps even in your dreams. Keep a journal of any dreams you have tonight and over the next few days, as they could be very meaningful.

Your Turn: Design Your Own Spread!

Now that you've become acquainted with some popular and widely used layouts as well as some spreads I've designed exclusively for this book, you may be thinking, "I can create my own layout too!" Yes, you can, and I encourage you to do so. You can call it anything your heart desires. Go for it! One of the things to keep in mind is to design a spread that you feel comfortable with and like doing. If there are many cards and too much "stuff" to memorize, you could become disenchanted with the entire process.

So to begin with, keep your own personalized spread short and simple. If you are an athlete, why not make up a sports spread that will reveal the outcome of a game? Maybe you'll get answers about the results of a future playoff tournament. Ask what you can do to improve your performance record. Let the focus be sports.

If much of your energy is spent on your friends, examine more deeply those close ties and other unique relationships. And everyone is curious about their love life! So think up some interesting questions you could ask the tarot about romance and maybe design the layout into the shape of a heart. There could be a spread that's titled "All about Me," and designed so the cards spell out your first name! There's no stopping you once your active imagination kicks in. So grab a notebook and pen and come up with some cool ideas to share with your friends and family. After you think up a list of intriguing questions and have associated each question with a different card position, design the layout and start reading your own personalized spread!

Developing Your Psychic Abilities

THE TAROT, JUST LIKE the runes and palmistry, is a tool to help you enhance your own psychic abilities. Everyone is born with an intuitive side, but some people have learned to use it more than others. Working with your tarot deck is one way you can increase your psychic powers. The deck gives you something on which to focus completely, thus allowing your mind to open up and "see" things.

Before you begin a reading you should make yourself completely comfortable. Sit in a cushy chair or lie down for a few minutes. If you know how to meditate this would be quite helpful too. If not, just relax and clear your mind. Let go of any nagging problems.

Turn your television and computer off. Make sure no one will disturb you as you prepare yourself to embrace a relaxed frame of mind. If you still feel anxious, then focus your mind on one object, like a pretty picture, a flower, or a tree outside your window.

Breathe in and out in a slow, relaxed manner. Once you feel calm, your mind will be ready to greet its intuitive side. Have your tarot deck ready to help you tap into this amazing power. You do not need to concern yourself with the traditional meaning of each tarot card now. In fact, I would prefer that you not refer to the book for any guidance at this time. Let your psychic antenna be your only guide. Shuffle the cards as you normally would before a reading. Stop shuffling when you "feel" the time is right. Take the top card from the deck and lay it down in front of you, picture side up. Now I want you to completely clear your mind and ask yourself, "What is this card trying to tell me? What is its message?" There are a few things to consider when you're reading the cards purely from an intuitive view.

1. How do you feel about the card? Does it make you happy, sad, anxious, upset, confused?

2. What is the very first thought that pops into your mind when you flip the card over? Go with that thought.

3. Now draw another card. How do you feel about it? If you are confused and feel as if you aren't getting anywhere or you are straining to get an answer, draw another card and go on. You can always come back to the difficult card and it may make more sense after you see what the rest of the layout is trying to show you.

4. Continue to draw as many cards as you like until you feel like stopping. I suggest you start out with ten cards at first and gradually build up to a higher number as you learn to work with your intuitive side.

5. Look for a particular theme to play out in the reading. Is there a specific message that keeps repeating itself?

6. Now, write down a few notes about your feelings and impressions from the cards. The first couple of times you

do a psychic tarot reading you may only get a few key words. But I promise, the more you read your deck in this manner, you will be amazed at how much information your higher self feeds you! You may have many pages of a notebook filled with messages.

7. Wait a few days or even a month and look back on the information you wrote down. How does it correspond with what has happened recently in your life? Did you gain any insight? The answer will likely be "Yes!"

8. Don't try to "intellectualize" the messages you receive. Go with your first thought or impression of each card. If you second guess your intuition, you will shut down the natural flow of information.

The Heart of the Tarot

IT'S TIME TO REALLY get into the heart of the tarot! Are you ready? We'll be examining each and every card in the deck for its meaning. Here within this chapter, you will unlock even more ancient wisdom. You can choose to memorize the meaning of each card, or you may refer to the book when you do a layout. Before long, you may not need to look up every card—you'll be an old pro at the art of tarot reading before you know it!

Each card description includes a picture of the card, a few keywords that will be easy to memorize, and an upright and reversed position description. The upright position means the card is facing you right side up. The reversed position means the card has been drawn upside down. If you draw a card upside down, you must leave it as is and read it that way, for it has a special and different meaning than its upright position. (Generally, the reversed position means the opposite, but not always!)

The Major Arcana

0. The Fool

Keywords: carefree, joy, travel, wanderlust,
confusion, change, adventure.

Upright Position

When you draw the Fool, you'll soon be enjoying a new
adventure! Yet another cycle of life is about to begin. Perhaps
you're enrolling in a different school, graduating, or starting
your first job. You'll have doubts about this new direction,
but don't hesitate or worry, everything will turn out in your
favor. Just heed your inner voice. This is an exciting period,
although there may be unexpected twists and turns. You
must take chances that seem risky if you want to get ahead.
Do you have a question or concern about your love life? Well,

a new relationship is right around the corner. On the job, apply for a top position. Your resume is top notch! It's kind of scary trying new things sometimes, isn't it? Learn to take more risks. I'm sure you'll be pleasantly surprised!

Reversed Position

Don't proceed with current plans. Be careful of what you say and do now. You may be coming to a fork in the road and could choose the wrong direction! There'll be a heavy price to pay if you rush into things without thinking about all of the options. At this time, unexpected delays and problems appear. This card reversed also foretells of foolish decisions amid lots of confusion. Don't cave into peer pressure. You'll feel bored and crave more excitement, but don't jump the gun. Understand that your current choices aren't the right ones. Be more cautious. Don't trust everyone, as so-called friends could lead you astray.

I. The Magician

Keywords: spiritual, magic, brilliant, preparation.

Upright Position

The Magician represents magical powers that we all possess. The power of your imagination and mind is very strong. Thoughts are like boomerangs. They come back to you. Send positive messages out into the universe. Speak only encouraging words. You have the ability now to manifest anything you want. You create your own destiny. Perhaps you're starting a project, competing in a new sport, or working toward a challenging goal. Like the Magician, you have extraordinary powers to make dreams come true and magic happen. For me, this is one of the best cards in the deck. It means you have the ability to achieve anything!

Reversed Position

People are not as sincere as they seem. Some of your friends are not true blue. Beware of two-faced acquaintances. They could be hidden enemies. Don't follow the wrong crowd just because the girls or boys appear to be cool or popular. Listen to your inner voice. Stay true to who you are. If you remain strong in your own belief system, things will run smoothly. You may miss out on a few golden opportunities because you lack confidence now, but this troubling period will pass soon. In the meantime, trust yourself more. Don't depend on others for advice. They could easily lead you down a dead-end road.

II. The High Priestess

Keywords: intuitive, mystery, occult, spiritual knowledge, psychic.

Upright Position

The High Priestess appears in your layout when you need to use your own psychic abilities. Trust your intuition now. It will not serve you wrong. Go with that gut feeling. This card also bears warning of a situation that's not what it appears to be. Deception is around you. Listen to your dreams too. They have much to reveal. If there's a problem or concern that's troubling you, know it may take an entire month to work itself out. Practice patience until then. In the meantime, this card will help spur an interest in the occult and could foretell of increased intuition on your part. The High Priestess will help the accuracy of your readings too.

Reversed Position

You're riding an emotional roller coaster ride. However, it's important that you remain calm. Don't get bent out of shape. This is not the time to act impulsively, as one may later regret actions taken. It seems everyone is "pulling your chain." Motto to live by: Remain cool, calm, and collected. You can't force an issue. Don't even try. A mysterious woman may enter your life, and she may mislead you! You'll want to give everyone the benefit of the doubt, but please take heed and be extra cautious with those in whom you place your trust.

III. The Empress

Keywords: fertility, mother, domestic, happiness.

Upright Position

You're close to reaching a goal! There's much to be proud of. The blue ribbon is yours. Luck is abundant in relationships, at school, or at work. Projects you initiate now flourish and grow. Your love life takes on a new twist . . . for the better! Take a look in the mirror. That lovely face smiling back is beautiful! You look fantastic and know it. Bottle all this self-confidence and go for the gold. This is also a card of fertility. Someone you know well could have a baby! The Empress also suggests a young mother or a woman of child-bearing years.

Reversed Position

There are road blocks everywhere you turn! You're working harder than ever but can't seem to get very far. Be patient, as this period will pass soon. Your efforts seem fruitless and very frustrating. It is of utmost importance to keep your chin up now. Believe in yourself even when reason for self-doubt lingers. In other words, don't give up. Have faith. Everything will turn out for the best!

IV. The Emperor

Keywords: strength, power, protection, authority, father.

Upright Position

The Emperor wants to share his great wisdom and insight regarding success. If you're wishing on a lucky star, dreams come true! Happiness is right around the corner. Don't delay or procrastinate. Move forward with courage and conviction. Doors will easily open. Love is yours for the taking. Yes, anything is possible now, especially if you are willing to work hard. Be thankful and graciously accept the blessings and opportunities the Emperor represents. This card also suggests that an older, authority male figure will help you.

Reversed Meaning

Have you been feeling a little down lately? Perhaps you're depressed or discouraged about something? Friends aren't as supportive as usual. You're at the end of your rope! This is a challenging period, one in which you won't get any easy breaks. You may apply for a job and not get hired. You may ask someone out on a date, only to face rejection. There is danger, frustration, and jealousy around. But you are determined and will learn just how strong you really are! If you feel your ideas and dreams are valid, stick with them. All problems will eventually work out.

V. The Hierophant

Keywords: wisdom, family, tradition,
compassion, rituals, strength.

Upright Position

Your answers do not come quickly through the Hierophant. Slow down. Play a waiting game. You are impatient and anxious for things to happen. You must create more order in everyday life so things can run smoothly. Stay with a regular routine. Don't try anything new right now. Actually, this is the perfect time to meditate. Look for answers deep within. If your question is about love, you need to either make a deeper commitment or break off the relationship. On the job, make sure communication is clear. This card is also telling you to get more rest. Go to bed earlier!

Reversed Position

In its reversed position, this card means nothing but chaos! You will feel challenged and want to break free. You're sick and tired of being dubbed a "goody two shoes." Life seems so boring! Close friendships now seem distant and aloof. Even though you're attracted now to the wilder side of life, you must remain cautious. You could be stepping into dangerous, uncharted territory. If you are unsure about something or someone right now, don't get involved.

VI. The Lovers

Keywords: relationships, love, choice, test, chemistry, sex.

Upright Position

Get ready to fall madly in love! Either a guy is already flirting with you or you have set your sights on a special someone. One way or another, you'll need to make an important decision regarding love very soon. Intuition will be strong. Use your heart rather than your head now. Sometimes, this card represents the return of an old flame. Regardless of the circumstance, you'll harbor strong feelings toward someone. A love affair that begins under this influence may lead to a serious commitment.

Reversed Position

The Lovers card reversed strongly suggests trouble ahead in your personal and intimate relationships. Things will not be easy and there will be a lot of miscommunication between you and your significant other. You may have to make a choice that you don't want to make. Expect rough roads ahead. If attached, there could be a breakup, tears, and sorrow. If single, you may face rejection or meet no one worthwhile. It's better to fly solo now.

VII. The Chariot

Keywords: competition, success, victory, rewards, conflict, travel.

Upright Position

Expect change when you draw the Chariot. If you've been struggling with a situation, you're able to break down barriers. There's freedom to move forward. You have learned a great deal in the past several weeks. For one thing, you've learned that nothing stays the same; so therefore, you must be open to accepting new opportunities. Past troubles are slipping away. The future lies before you, filled with the possibilities of new friends, job opportunities, a different school, or a major move. Travel could be on your agenda too. Expect to take a pleasant trip.

Reversed Position

If you're planning a trip, it may get canceled. Don't be disappointed. You will be able to take it another time. This is also a period in which you are feeling a little down. Perhaps your self-confidence is low. Maybe you feel rejected. This will pass. It's not a favorable period in which to make important decisions or start a project. Things won't work out as planned. This time is best used to meditate. Listen to your inner voice. Things will improve in a few short weeks.

VIII. Strength

Keywords: power, courage, defeat of evil forces, integrity.

Upright Position

You'll resolve any problems that come your way in no time flat. Just be sure to use a gentle touch rather than force. Remember the old saying, "You can catch more flies with honey?" Same goes for your current situation. Be extra patient and kind to friends and family. The Strength card is also urging you to be kind to yourself. Homework, chores, and extracurricular activities have been keeping you busy. You can't catch up on sleep, but please try! It's important that you balance play with work now. Your confidence soars, and if there are any difficulties, you'll move through them with ease.

Reversed Position

This card reversed means you are feeling tired and down. Time is ripe for catching a cold or the flu. Your energy levels may be low, so take extra care now. Load up on vitamin C and get more rest. Try not to overdo it. Prioritize your time and make sure you get to bed at a decent hour every night. There may be many difficult and demanding people around. Don't let them bother you. The energy you spend arguing is not worth it.

IX. The Hermit

Keywords: isolation, solitude, renewal,
self-awareness, sacrifice, spirituality.

Upright Position

This card suggests that you're coming out of a period of
great activity and restlessness. Now is the time to let your
body rest for a while. Answers to problems will not come
right away, and therefore you'll feel frustrated. The best
thing to do is retreat into your own world. Rest, relaxation,
and solitude help rejuvenate your spirit. The Hermit represents the "inner self," and by getting in touch with it, solutions to problems come easily and light your way. If you feel
a need to talk over concerns, a school counselor or trusted
friend would be beneficial at this time.

Reversed Position

The Hermit is warning you to be extra careful. Take time to heed your inner voice. The universe is trying to send you messages. Meditate. Slow down and breathe. Teachers and parents are giving good advice, but you may not want to accept it. You could get angry, upset, and reject offers of help, even from best friends. But you must not turn them away. Those who want to help are truly guardian angels. Listen to them. Know that you are not alone and any problems are easily resolved.

X. The Wheel of Fortune

Keywords: the four seasons, cycles, luck, opportunities, fate, destiny, redirection.

Upright Position

Spin the Wheel of Fortune and see what lands in your lap. You are especially lucky now. One cycle of your life has just ended. You're ready to embark on a new one, filled with amazing opportunities and blessings. Expect good things to come your way. Be open to taking risks and making changes. You will be amazed at all of the wonderful things that are manifesting. New relationships, exciting projects, and interests await you. The wheel is turning in a positive direction. Trust that everything will turn out even better than expected, and that things designed for your highest good will come to fruition .

Reversed Position

Here, the Wheel of Fortune brings a reversal of luck. There's a sense of going backward or not moving forward at all. Nothing seems to be working out. It's as if a dark cloud is looming overhead. Delays and frustrations are evident, but things do not stay this way for long. Know that this is a temporary state of being. It's not a favorable time for starting anything new. New relationships and activities just won't pan out. Play a waiting game. Put everything on hold, if you can, for a few weeks.

XI. Justice

Keywords: law, reward and punishment, balance, fairness.

Upright Position

Whatever you put out will come back to you! Be honest and fair in all dealings. Treat everyone like you want to be treated. If involved in a legal matter, things will turn in your favor. Sometimes this card foretells of an impending marriage, a new relationship, or an engagement. Promises of love and devotion are highlighted. Also, you may be discovering more about your own needs in relationships and friendships. Any problems or concerns will work out, but may take a few weeks. The outcome will be fair. You needn't worry about being taken advantage of. Justice will prevail in the long run.

Reversed Position

Things are not fair. You may feel victimized by someone or a situation. You probably are. Some people may be working against your goals and desires. Be careful of hidden enemies. A few appear to be friends but are really two-faced. On a mundane level, if you are driving, be extra careful because you could get a speeding ticket. Avoid getting after-school detention and suspensions. You may not get the grades you think you deserve on a report card. Some things will seem so unfair. Friends will argue more. Parents are on your case. Don't fight back because it may make matters worse.

XII. The Hanged Man

Keywords: sacrifice, suffering, renewal,
final difficulty, ordeal, transition.

Upright position

The Hanged Man represents sadness and sacrifice. You may end a relationship, cut ties with a friend, or give up on a goal you once considered important. However, an ending will not be as terrible as you might think. You may also feel in "limbo," waiting for a situation to change or for something to happen. Life is a little boring now. Do something creative: draw, dance, sing, or write. Creativity will help you through this confusing period. The important thing to remember is that what you're experiencing now will pass within a few days or weeks. You can learn a lot from what you're going through. Keeping a journal of your thoughts can help too.

Reversed Position

The Hanged Man reversed is actually a good omen. It basically means there's an end in sight. No more frustration, suffering, or crises. Many of your questions will be answered. People are nicer. Barriers are broken down. What once was held back is now yours. Ready for change? Impatient? Don't be. Things are moving forward again. There's a sense of freedom. You win!

XIII. Death

Keywords: change, transformation, sudden changes, fear, regeneration.

Upright Position

The Death card upright means a positive change in your current condition. You're dropping bad habits and possibly letting go of negative friends and activities. This is the beginning of a new life for you. Your belief system will change a bit. Many new and wonderful opportunities await you. Press forward. You must let go of the past and be open to what the future holds in store. Soon, there will be much to celebrate. In other words, the final result will be very welcome.

Reversed Position

The Death card reversed foretells of a crisis that you can't seem to overcome. You may be the cause of the problem. Perhaps it is you who may not want to let go of something that is negative. Are you repressing your true feelings? Are you afraid to let go? We sometimes hang on to old beliefs and sour thinking from time to time. You could be afraid to leave a negative peer group or drop an addiction. Fear is what is holding you back. If one is open to "letting go," things will change for the better.

(Note: People often assume that the Death card's meaning is negative. Many feel this card literally means a physical death, that someone close to them is going to die, or that they will die. Some beginners assume it's the worst card in the entire deck. Not so! The Death card merely means a major change is coming. You may not like the change initially, but the outcome will be quite positive.)

XIV. Temperance

Keywords: patience, serenity, peace,
understanding, self-control.

Upright Position

Are you ready to receive all of the wonderful blessings your angels wish to bring you? Your hard work is now complete. You've gone through a period of turmoil and crisis. It's time to be rewarded. However, if something seems to be missing in your life, or if there's a feeling of emptiness, it won't last much longer. When you draw this card, you can land the perfect job, discover new friends, and even meet your soul mate! If you were depressed in the past, there was a reason for it. Now, you've reached a point where you can appreciate what the world has to offer. Soon, life will be in perfect harmony and balance.

Reversed Position

You're trying to accomplish too much, too soon. Therefore, nothing gets done. You'll burn out before long if you don't slow down. This could be a difficult time filled with many challenges. However, these tests make you stronger. The way you look at life and your belief system may change a lot too. Reevaluate what you are doing and the path you are taking. Don't repeat the same mistakes over and over again. Stop this cycle before it's too late to turn things around.

XV. The Devil

Keywords: deceit, negative energy, betrayal, lies, manipulation, excess, selfishness.

Upright Position

You could become obsessed with someone, to the point that it's not healthy. You may feel frightened about something too. Many times, fear comes from being overzealous. Maybe you're dating someone and fear a breakup is coming. It may be for the best, but you won't let go of this dying love affair. Perhaps you're obsessed with making money. Don't take on more jobs than you can handle. Your school work will suffer. This card affirms that true and total happiness only comes from within. When the Devil card comes up in a spread, understand that you could make a wrong choice. Do not use, manipulate, hurt, or deceive anyone. Lies will come back to haunt you!

Reversed Position

The reversed Devil card is actually a good omen. There's a breakthrough in current conditions. You have just come out of a struggling period. Now is the time to bask in the winner's circle. No one can hold you back. It's easy to walk away from a bad relationship. Say adios to a two-faced friend and learn from past mistakes. Be confident that things are changing for the better. Soon you will experience love, laughter, and light once again!

XVI. The Tower

Keywords: destruction, explosives, devastation, disruption, unexpected problems.

Upright Position

Expect the unexpected. The Tower card warns that dramatic changes are about to occur. Stress or confusion may have been building up over a period of time to create a major explosion. The change itself will happen quickly. You could break a relationship off, quit a job without giving notice, or have a blowup with your best friend. Expect upheaval. You will be anxious. At least you are forewarned. When the dust settles, you'll have a better understanding and idea of why this chaos had to happen. There are many lessons to learn. Things will not stay the same.

Reversed Position

Do you feel as if something exciting is about to happen? You sense a change is near but are not sure when the change will come. The reversed Tower confirms that, yes, there is an upheaval, but it is expected. You can accept and manage the outcome well. Even though there will be some surprises over the next few weeks, you'll be able to handle them. This could actually be a very productive phase of your life. Be open to accepting change. It's usually for the best.

XVII. The Star

Keywords: hope, blessing, opportunity, beauty, wishes come true.

Upright Position

Wish upon a star and expect your dreams to come true! This card tells you to expect many new and exciting adventures. If you've been upset about something, a change is occurring for the better. Expect good to come to you. Friends are supportive and loyal. If you need help in any area of your life, don't be afraid to ask, because many will come to your aid. Once closed, doors of opportunity now open. People love and adore you! This is a great time to show off. Enter contests, talent shows, and competitions.

Reversed Position

Reversed, the Star foretells of indecisiveness and doubt. Have you lost all faith in yourself? Do you feel bored and as if life is meaningless? If so, don't worry, for this is only a temporary state of mind. You can use spiritual tools to get through this period. Try meditating, use uplifting affirmations, and do something creative. This dark cloud will lift, but you must push yourself to keep going. Understand that it's your choice to smile or frown. If you smile, the light within you will glow and things turn around much more quickly. Do not allow yourself to hold a pity party.

XVIII. The Moon

Keywords: dreams, curiosity, deception, gossip, illusions, infatuation.

Upright Position

Your psychic antennas are tuned in! You know exactly who's on the other end of the phone when it rings! Your sixth sense is working overtime. Listen closely to revealing insights. Sometimes the Moon card suggests you're overwhelmed by life. Beware of deceitful people. Friends could be gossiping behind your back. There are a lot of rumors floating around. The moon's phases take one month, so don't expect changes to happen for thirty days. You'll need lots of your energy to deal with negativity. Listen to your intuition, but get advice from others too, as it may be hard to understand your own subconscious messages or visions right now.

Reversed Position

There's a sense that everything is going to be all right. The turmoil around you is coming to an end. No longer will you experience the deception you've had to face in the past from so-called friends. If someone is lying to you, you'll be able to see the "truth" quite clearly. The darkness is turning into light. You are in control and can now move forward with lots of enthusiasm and determination. Don't let anything stand in your way. Use your intuition. It won't serve you wrong.

XIX. The Sun

Keywords: fame, happiness, growth, progress, security.

Upright Position

Everything is bright and sunny! Success is yours for the taking. However, you need to take the first steps to achieve your goals and desires. Have a new idea you want to run with? Go for it! You'll experience bursts of energy and excitement. You cannot fail! The world is waiting for you. It's granting your every wish. Use this time to make progress and to make your dreams come true. Don't delay. You'll feel safe and secure. Every path you take will lead to a happy ending. Relationships bloom. There are no roadblocks or obstacles standing in your way. Whenever you see the Sun card, you should feel positive and know that you're moving forward.

Reversed Position

There's a sense of defeat surrounding your efforts. A goal or project you've been dedicated to doesn't work out as you had envisioned. Someone else may take credit for your work. You won't get the recognition you deserve. Somebody may purposely block you from getting ahead. Your time to reap reward is coming, but it's not now, so keep the faith. Avoid getting depressed. Erase any negative thoughts. This is a temporary setback, so don't allow yourself to give up on long-term goals. Just play a waiting game.

XX. Judgment

Keywords: challenges, news, decisions in your favor,
culmination, fulfillment, fairness.

Upright Position

This is a final decision card. You'll be making your mind up
very soon about something. If you've had your share of troubles and misfortunes in the past, these difficult times are
soon over. Much progress can be made now. The choices that
lie before you are quite clear. If you're willing to release old
fears, then wonderful changes can occur. Nothing, absolutely
nothing, is impossible now. But remember, you are the one
that calls the shots. Think before you act.

Reversed Position

You may feel as if the dream you are chasing is not within your reach. Perhaps the road you're on is leading nowhere. Discouragement is all around you. This is a time to review your goals, but don't allow negative thinking to hold you back. You may be on the wrong path. These goals may be too far-fetched. Bring them down to reality. There is a season and reason for everything. The stars are a strong guiding influence. Don't give up. Just change your course of action. Readjust.

XXI. The World

Keywords: reward, happiness, success, contentment.

Upright Position

Congratulations! You have come full circle. Things couldn't be any better. The wisdom you have gained will be put to good use. This is a period of achievement, recognition, and reward. Perhaps you've made the honor roll, are graduating, or have aced a difficult exam. There's a lot to be excited about. Now reward is yours. It's all due to hard work and perseverance. Take control of your life and enjoy all of the things the world has to offer. This is your "dance of life" card. So go on ahead and "boogie" all night long!

Reversed Position

As this cycle of your life comes to an end, you will experience frustration and delay. Yes, there will be endings, and some of them you're sure to dislike. Face the fact that life is changing. You could be going off to college but feel homesick. Perhaps you're transferring to a new school. You may be moving. Whatever the change, there will be a sense of loss along with it. This card foretells the end of a friendship or romantic involvement. Change is inevitable. Roll with the punches. You'll be stronger in the long run.

Minor Arcana

Ace of Cups

Keywords: abundance, love, happiness.

Upright Position

Love is knocking at your back door. It may be where you least expect to find it too. However, the Ace of Cups only foretells of a potential relationship, not the result of it. So, if you find yourself fantasizing about someone, it may be up to you to initiate the first move. Take charge. Go after the guy or girl of your dreams. This is also a very spiritual card. It's telling you to listen to your inner voice. It will guide you when it comes to making important decisions involving matters of the heart.

Reversed Position

Your love life stinks! Either there are no decent prospects in sight or there's turmoil in a current relationship. You're likely feeling alone and withdrawn. Don't allow yourself to indulge in pity parties. Keep the faith. Meditate more. Ask your angels and spirit guides what it is you are supposed to learn during this somber period. If a relationship is at its breaking point, let it go sooner rather than later.

Two Of Cups

Keywords: marriage, commitment, passion, choice.

Upright Position

Is it fate? Is it destiny? Could it be true love? You've drawn the "soul mate" card. Yes, you're on the verge of meeting a soul mate. At the very least, a destined relationship is coming in. Soon, you'll share a special bond with someone who's love is unconditional. Has someone recently appeared in your life? Did you meet a new person the other day to whom you felt a strong connection? New people you meet this month could be a source of inspiration and the beginning of a beautiful thing.

Reversed Position

Beware of problems in a close relationship. They could possibly lead to a permanent breakup. Trouble is brewing because one of you is acting foolish and immature. Even if your relationship appears stable now, it is shaky. It has the potential to fall apart when you least expect it. Don't cause any arguments or upsets that you'll come to regret down the road. If you've suppressed feelings and not dealt with problems in the past, they'll come back to haunt you now.

Three of Cups

Keywords: celebration, appreciation, happy endings.

Upright Position

There's so much to be thankful for over the next few weeks. Expect much happiness and joy. Creative pursuits are favored. You'll feel as if you're part of a winning team. You may get invited to a wonderful party or a celebration you won't want to miss. Enjoy your successes, as there will be many. Friends and family are happy for you too. Make sure to make time for everyone. The Three of Cups signifies birthdays, anniversaries, and all sorts of reasons to throw a great party!

Reversed Position

Count your blessings. Don't envy others, but rather be thankful for what you have achieved in your own life. Don't let the green-eyed monster come between you and others. You're likely to be quite envious of a friend's success. It's only because yours is delayed in coming. The universe's delay is not its denial. You will succeed. Even though you haven't made it to the winner's circle just yet, the sweet smell of victory is not far off. Try to express enthusiasm and joy for a pal's happiness.

Four of Cups

Keywords: creation, boredom, refuse.

Upright Position

When the Four of Cups falls anywhere in your spread, it brings a stern warning: There's much love in your life, but if taken for granted, that love will slip away. However, it's not too late. You still have time to make positive changes in your love life or friendship circle. Appreciate others and let them know how much they mean to you. This is a time to give love as well as receive it. The more you give, the more you get back. Shower family and friends with compliments, hugs, and kisses.

Reversed Position

Close, personal relationships prove disappointing now. Perhaps you are expecting too much from other people. Be careful of a demanding or selfish attitude. Sometimes, the Four of Cups reversed means that a close friend will disappoint you by acting arrogant and egotistical. If a relationship is broken, it's repairable, but only if both parties take responsibility for any problems.

Five of Cups

Keywords: conflict, change, loss, fear.

Upright Position

Even though you may be headed for a breakup in a relationship, there's still time to reverse things. There is hope. It's time to change your course of action and mend some fences. It's going to take patience on your part to overcome obstacles, but it can be done! Don't worry about things you can't change. Let go of the past. Concentrate only on the future. If you cling to old wounds, habits, and patterns, you won't succeed. Build the relationship from the ground up again. Only then will it flourish and grow.

Reversed Position

A sense of sadness prevails. Have you recently experienced the breakup of a meaningful relationship? If the answer is yes, you should let go. It's likely it won't work out anyway, and the relationship has run its course. If you refuse to bid farewell and hang on, you're only postponing true happiness. In time, you will see why this ending had to occur. It's for your own good, even though you can't see through your tears. Have a good cry and move on!

Six of Cups

Keywords: the past, sentimental, memories.

Upright Position

Your heart is hurting. You felt it break in two. A relationship you once had high hopes for has ended. But don't despair, because you are headed into a period of great reward and happiness. There's a precious opportunity or gift coming your way. You'll be surprised. Things are moving forward. No longer will you be a prisoner of the past. The Six of Cups also suggests fertility, children, sex, and childhood. There's a new path opening up to you. Allow your heart to accept the new romantic possibilities that await you.

Reversed Position

Are you stuck between the past and the present? Do you feel you can't move forward? What's holding you back from finding true happiness? Let go of the disappointment and sadness of recent weeks. Refuse to focus on disappointments. No longer will you look back, only forward. The past is over. Today is a gift. That's why they call it the present. Open your gift and be grateful you have opportunities to create change. If you have faith in yourself, everything will turn out better than expected.

Seven of Cups

Keywords: daydreaming, imagination, variety.

Upright Position

You may be going through a period in which you can't make a decision. There may be several people to whom you feel attracted. Which one should you choose? You will be asked to decide between two love interests. At least you have options! Both are tempting. In fact, temptation is the main theme of this card. You will make the right choice if you follow your intuition. This is also a good card for any type of creative work. You'll find yourself getting caught up in daydreams too!

Reversed Position

You should weigh your decisions very carefully now. Think before you act. You'll be tempted to jump to conclusions without having all of the facts. This creates more chaos, leaving yourself open to disappointment. Be wary of people or circumstances that appear too good to be true. They probably are! Your judgment is not good, so only seek advice from people you trust.

Eight of Cups

Keywords: education, knowing, immaturity, evaluation.

Upright Position

The past is gone with the wind. Things cannot be changed at this point. Only the future lies before you. An important relationship has ended. Or perhaps it's just a matter of time until it's over. However, you can expect someone new to come into your life. He or she wishes to invite you on a magical journey. This will be a period of amazing self-discovery. You're being encouraged to unlock hidden talents and perhaps your spiritual side. If you have let go of an old dream or goal, a new one is coming to replace it. When one door closes, another opens.

Reversed Position

You'll be asked to make sacrifices that you don't want to make. Even though life doesn't seem fair now, there's a reason your current situation is in a state of flux. Don't act impulsively. You don't have all of the answers just yet. In time you'll know exactly what it is you are supposed to do. Trust that the universe has your best interest at heart, and all will turn out just fine.

Nine of Cups

Keywords: satisfaction, contentment, fulfillment.

Upright Position

You have drawn one of the most uplifting and positive cards in the entire tarot deck. You'll feel at peace in more ways than one: emotionally, physically, mentally, and spiritually. Known also as the Wish card, the Nine of Cups is offering a chance to do just that. Close your eyes now and make a wish. Watch it come true. Give love and get it back threefold. Whatever your heart desires shall be granted. Rest assured you will get what you need, even though it may not be exactly as you expect. The Wish card brings opportunity for your highest good.

Reversed Position

"Caution" is your key word now. Don't overindulge in anything. You could get sick. Watch your diet. Get plenty of rest. Your patience may be tested too. If you try to force an issue or take things to the extreme, you may suffer disappointment. If there are any roadblocks in your life, you must learn to go around them or over them, not through them. If you are pushy or arrogant now, you'll undoubtedly lose a few friends.

Ten of Cups

Keywords: happiness, positive results,
family harmony, resistance.

Upright Position

The Ten of Cups brings much happiness. There is an abundance of good luck all around you. If you're working on a goal, know that you'll achieve it. Enjoy your moment in the spotlight. If true love is your wish, it's right around the bend. Both you and the object of your affection will be filled with the power of love. Use this special time to create more peace and harmony in your relationships.

Reversed Position

Don't cop a negative attitude or go looking for problems. You'll find yourself on the losing end of a proposition. It's as if you're making the same mistakes over and over again. A sense of fear or failure may overcome you. Yet there really is nothing to fear. Don't be afraid to pursue a relationship or reveal your true feelings. If you don't take a chance on love, you could lose out on a wonderful opportunity!

Page of Cups

Keywords: news, communication, new ideas, information.

Upright Position

When you draw this card, expect a very special person to come into your life. There's a special reason for his or her appearance too. This person is a true romantic at heart, and may also be artistic and creative. This unique individual is here to help you grow stronger in your spiritual beliefs. He or she will offer words of wisdom as well as love and compassion. The unusual encounter may seem to have a fated quality about it. Expect the unexpected to happen now. Someone wants to create a positive change in your life!

Reversed Position

You may feel a bit lonely. Perhaps you are depressed. Life seems boring. Even though it's hard to get motivated you shouldn't waste time sitting around whining! This dark time will pass. Your subconscious is trying to send you messages. Be aware of what the tarot is trying to tell you. Dreams may be significant at this time too. Whatever you do, don't give up. What you are experiencing is only a temporary setback.

Knight of Cups

Keywords: encouragement, seduction, invitation.

Upright Position

This Knight brings extra special news: invitations, proposals, parties, and messages of amour. Sometimes, he plays matchmaker and introduces you to a new relationship. Other times, the Knight creates a new project to work on. A friendship is developing too. If you meet someone under his influence, the person is probably a big flirt! Nonetheless, you'll feel very passionate about any new encounter. You won't need nearly as much encouragement to get a fire started. You could fall head over heels in love!

Reversed Position

Don't wear your heart on your sleeve over the next few weeks, or it could get broken. Be realistic in love. If you find you're becoming obsessed with someone, try to focus energies elsewhere; otherwise, your school work and daily routine could suffer. You may waste a lot of precious time longing for someone who isn't worth the effort and attention.

Queen of Cups

Keywords: wife, loyalty, good friend,
psychic, understanding.

Upright Position

This is one of the best tarot cards for psychic development.
The only card that beats it is the High Priestess. When you
draw the Queen of Cups, you're being asked to tap into your
higher self and unlock these intuitive powers. You'll also find
yourself comforting distraught friends. Giving advice and
showing compassion to those you care about may take a lot
of time and energy. There may be a woman or a mother-figure
who is helping you through a difficult situation as well.

Reversed Position

Don't believe everything you hear. Think with your head, not your heart. You may get too attached to someone or obsessed with an idea or dream. It's not a favorable period to make any long-term decisions either. Balance your logic and emotions, or unjustified fears take over and you'll be paranoid about silly things. Situations and people are not as intimidating as they seem. Don't overreact.

King of Cups

Keywords: protection, husband, father, creative.

Upright Position

The King of Cups offers you a peaceful, loving way to solve any problems that arise now. There could be a great new relationship forming with a mysterious man. He speaks from the heart. He's also a romantic at heart and wishes to extend his kindness to you. You can learn much from this King, so keep an ear open to the wisdom he wants to share. If you need support with a problem or assistance completing a difficult project, you'll get help.

Reversed Position

Be forewarned! There's a man coming into your life that could be extremely selfish. Safeguard your heart! He's a liar and a manipulator. He only cares about getting his way and is quite egotistical. When you first meet, you'll feel very drawn to him. But after time, his ulterior motives may become evident and you could emotionally get hurt. If you already know this man, it is best to end the relationship immediately. Also, make sure not to blame others for any disappointments you may suffer now. You may have made bad choices, and must now own up to them.

Ace of Pentacles

Keywords: success, gain, good news.

Upright Position

Expect fame and fortune! The spotlight is shining on you. All of your hard work and effort pays off. Events turn in your favor. Be ready to take a giant leap. The Ace of Pentacles brings presents and proposals. Don't sit back and daydream about what you'd like to do. Now's the time to take action. Make those dreams come true! If you've been waiting for an announcement or decision, the news will be good. Apply for a job, loan, or scholarship. Folks tend to appreciate your effort and talents more than ever.

Reversed Position

You've hit a roadblock. Open your eyes and see what's really going on around you. You could be missing the boat. Goals and projects that you've started may take longer now to achieve and finish. Take time to ask yourself, "Are these goals for my highest good?" If you can honestly answer "Yes," then go forward with plans. If the answer is "No," then it's best to start over on a new path or you could waste a lot of precious time.

Two of Pentacles

Keywords: boredom, uneasiness, abundance.

Upright Position

Your financial picture is changing . . . for the better. So take life a little easier and make time to play. You've probably been studying and working hard lately. The same old routine is growing dull. Get out and have some fun. This card suggests that you have several projects going at once. Activities at school? Sports groups? Church interests? Maybe you've started a new hobby. Remember how important it is to plan your time wisely. Two of Pentacles gives you an opportunity to expand your horizons. However, you must make time to relax or you'll burn out!

Reversed Position

You need to make necessary changes in your routine now. If you do not, things could fall apart. Personal spending habits need some review too, or you'll find yourself broke. There's never enough money to go around. Two of Pentacles reversed suggests there are too many irons in the fire. Therefore, you may not excel at anything you set out to do. Slow down. Create a balance and you'll find more peace and harmony in everyday life.

Three of Pentacles

Keywords: discovery, decisions made, exploring.

Upright Position

A reward for your efforts is forthcoming. If there's a goal that truly inspires you, you'll achieve it. Get excited about the future because it looks bright. You are mastering something. It could be a foreign language, a new skill, or a talent. This card tells us that with hard work and determination, any goal is possible to reach. You could be on the threshold of an amazing discovery about yourself. The decisions you make now will be beneficial to you, even years from now.

Reversed Position

Be careful and act responsibly in all of your dealings. You must stick to daily schedules and routines. Follow all rules and procedures. If you ignore these things, more problems prevail. Now is a good time to look over your current conditions. Are you bored? Confused? Misunderstood? If you feel any of these things, the best way to shake discouragement is to keep busy. Get a part-time job, enroll in a sports program, or take an art class. Fill your hours and stick to a regular routine. That'll help create a balance in your life.

Four of Pentacles

Keywords: greedy, gain, money.

Upright Position

Expect more money to come your way, probably through a generous family member or a new job. Perhaps you're already working. Now is the time to request a raise. But don't be too greedy! You'll lose money just as easily as it's gained if you're not careful. This card also hints at a possible inheritance, allowance, or extra blessings. Look for money that is promised. Shopping for new clothes and updating your look is especially important to you at this time.

Reversed Position

This is the money "karma" card. By this, I mean that if you act greedy and selfish, you will pinch pennies for awhile. There won't be enough money to do the things you want to do. You're being warned. Don't be greedy! If you treat others fairly, are kind and giving, your life will prosper. So will your pocketbook! Regarding relationships, if you are egotistical or arrogant, you'll lose a few friends and gain an enemy.

Five of Pentacles

Keywords: loss, struggle, problems, financial difficulties.

Upright Position

There's a strong warning associated with this card; you may experience a loss of some kind. More than likely, it's financial. It could very well be that a cherished friendship is ending too. And try as you might, you can't stop it from happening. However, if you've already been dealt a blow, know that you can change things for the better. There's still time to rectify the situation. In other words, there's hope. Use your intuition as a guide.

Reversed Position

Look for a reversal of misfortune. Have you experienced a loss of any kind? Are you disappointed with a financial deal? Has a relationship gone sour? Perhaps you weren't recognized for a job well done? Don't worry. Things are now turning around in your favor. All will be fine. Be still and listen to what your inner voice is telling you. Trust that all of your concerns are melting away. A resolution to a problem or sticky situation is close.

Six of Pentacles

Keywords: generous, gifts, presents, charity.

Upright Position

Be generous now, for the universe is asking that you give of yourself. You have learned so very much over the past few months. Perhaps you've recently come through a difficult time. Your faith has been tested. Now the universe is calling upon you to help the less fortunate. If there's a friend in need, take time to console him or her. Perhaps an elderly relative needs company. Do some volunteer work. Remember, the best gift you can give someone you love is the gift of your presence. Be there!

Reversed Position

Someone offers a helping hand. This person hopes to take a heavy burden off your shoulders. Let him or her assist you. Others are offering good advice. Listen to them. You're frustrated and shouldn't try to tackle problems alone. You need help. Karma is everywhere you turn. Paybacks can be positive or negative. Whatever you put out comes back to you. If you've helped others in the past, this is your time to receive. If you ignore their generosity, you may feel even more helpless.

Seven of Pentacles

Keywords: goal, achievement, results.

Upright Position

You should be very proud of yourself. You've been reaching for a goal and now it is at hand. Sometimes the best part of striving for something is the journey and the experiences you gain on your climb upward. Some people feel a letdown after they've reached their destination. If this is what you're feeling, you may need to reevaluate your goals. If most of the fun was "getting to the top," then it's time to come up with a new game plan. Decide what it is you'd like to conquer next. Begin reaching for another ideal. You have luck on your side. Don't be satisfied and stop now. Luck like this doesn't come around that often. Use the energy of this positive card to make dreams come true!

Reversed Position

There's a letdown. You may be disappointed. After all, you've worked very hard and thought you were headed in the right direction. But something or someone has stopped you dead in your tracks. Step back. Take a rest. Rethink strategies. After time you will see things clearly again. The main thing to remember is not to give up. This is just a phase you are going through. Mistakes made now are part of the learning process.

Eight of Pentacles

Keywords: dedication, commitment.

Upright Position

All your hard work seems fruitless. There's been little or no payoff. It will come. After all, you've shown a lot of dedication to a project and it is nearing completion now. The recognition you deserve will come, but not until the very end of the process. The Eight of Pentacles guarantees success, but you must pass all of the tests before it can be yours. If you've shown great commitment to a relationship, project, or goal, many rewards will come from your efforts. Your determination will prove worthwhile.

Reversed Position

Heed the advice of your family and friends now. They are trying to encourage you not to give up on an important goal. Consider them your personal cheerleaders. They have much faith in your abilities, and you should too! If you get discouraged and quit too soon, there is inevitable failure ahead. Please let others help you. If you fly solo and won't accept guidance or help, there will be many disappointments.

Nine of Pentacles

Keywords: well-being, security, money.

Upright Position

Life seems so perfect! The choices you've recently made are positive ones. Look for a windfall of some sort; perhaps an inheritance or a large gift of money. Someone may buy you an expensive present. You could receive a scholarship if you apply for one. With extra money at your disposal, spend wisely but enjoy this newfound wealth. You will be full of energy too, and quite healthy. Any type of exercise routine, diet, or self-improvement course is highly favored at this time.

Reversed Position

Safeguard your things. Don't let friends borrow clothes or special items—they could lose or damage them. The Nine of Pentacles reversed means a loss of some kind. You may feel broke. There's no extra cash coming in. You're scraping pennies together. Be patient. This is a temporary situation. Pick up part-time jobs if you can to tide you over.

Ten of Pentacles

Keywords: home and family, talents.

Upright Position

The universe will soon call on you to aid others. You possess wonderful talents and skills, and will be asked to share them. This is a good idea. You will prosper and grow as a person every time you reach out to people. Volunteer at a local shelter. Teach a younger child a skill. Share advice with a friend. Whatever you put out comes back to you—threefold. You have recently gone through a period of realization. Now try to come up with a way to use the knowledge you've gained to guide others. Home and family life looks excellent too!

Reversed Position

There is a danger of being too greedy. Don't forget about what's really important in your life . . . spiritual wealth. If you put too much emphasis on material things and money, you may experience a downfall. Recognize that money isn't everything. Even if you are lucky financially, be careful of making money your God. The universal law of money is that it travels in circles. Spend it. Share it. Donate to a charity. Then your wealth will expand.

Page of Pentacles

Keywords: study, ability, opportunity, talent.

Upright Position

You are on the verge of landing a dream job! There's a promotion or good news coming very soon. Many opportunities seem to just drop out of the sky and into your lap. You're ready to accept any responsibilities that come your way. Working toward a goal excites you. Look over all of the options presented and see which bring the most results. A new path opens up. A messenger brings good news.

Reversed Position

A problem with money arises. You will be disappointed. Perhaps you are not getting the raise or allowance you expected. Anticipated funds dry up. Your savings account is dwindling too. It's not a good idea to lend friends money either, unless you consider it a gift. They won't pay the debt, and it may cost you the friendship as well. Don't count your chickens before they are hatched, as there is a tendency to overspend and regret your purchases later.

Knight of Pentacles

Keywords: responsibility, service, helping others.

Upright Position

A crisis may arise in which you'll be required to take charge of a frustrating situation. Don't despair, for this Knight is here to help you. His offer may come unexpectedly. If you promise to do something, make sure to fulfill your obligations to others. Commitments are very important now and should be taken seriously. Act honestly. You are gaining the respect of a lot of people, some who are looking to you for guidance and leadership. Don't let them down.

Reversed Position

The lazy bug is biting! You're headed into a period where you feel unmotivated and downright bored with life. You must own up to responsibility now. However, there's a strong indication that you will act foolishly. Things are not as they appear. Your reputation could be at stake, as many people are gossiping about you. Expectations are high and will probably not be met. Disappointment and pressures are mounting unless you recognize you have the ability to create a positive change.

Queen of Pentacles

Keywords: generosity, kindness, devotion, goals, magnificence.

Upright Position

This is the Mother card. If it falls in your layout, expect a caring, maternal woman to come into your life to help you. She could be a teacher, a new friend, a boss, a coworker, or even your own mom. At times, this card shows that you are "mothering" someone else. Whatever the case, maternal instincts are high. You are generous and kind. Know that you have a direct link with a powerful spiritual energy. With a positive attitude, you can accomplish any goals you have set for yourself.

Reversed Position

A dangerous obsession, directed toward another person, may overcome you. It's unhealthy. Value yourself more. Self-confidence and self-esteem are low now. Don't allow yourself to fall into a trap of becoming a victim in a relationship. Stand firm in your beliefs. Do not let failures or discouraging remarks from others keep you down. Stay clear of negative people.

King of Pentacles

Keywords: success, devotion, expansion, foundation, intelligent.

Upright Position

You have the Midas touch. Everything turns to gold! Your success is due in part to the good karma you have laid over the past several months. You deserve happiness and rich blessings because of the kindness you have shown to others. Expect good things to come your way now. Be open to expanding your interests and horizons. Like a devoted and loving father, the King of Pentacles is here to support you in anything you set out to do. With his help, you can't go wrong!

Reversed Position

Don't expect miracles to happen. You're working very hard and burning the candle at both ends. It seems you're getting nowhere, and just about the time you do reach the top, everything comes crashing down! Part of the problem is you've put too much faith in people who aren't worthy of your trust. Someone, likely a man, has been giving you bad advice. He appeared trustworthy at first, but now it's clear this man has been misleading you all along.

Ace of Swords

Keywords: power, strength, winning.

Upright Position

Take the initiative. Exciting projects that you start will prove fulfilling, but only if you allow your inner wisdom and intuition to shine through. Let it work for you! Remember to always use your talents and skills in a positive way. If you misuse your power to hurt or manipulate others, the "magic" could be taken away from you. Don't manipulate or lie to get your way. Be honest in all of your dealings. Doors are opening. Problems are solved. This is a time you can break free from the past. Any self-doubt will be washed away. You have tapped into some amazing energy. Use it only for the highest good of everyone involved.

Reversed Position

Someone is misusing and abusing his or her personal power. If it is you, don't try to force your way or control others. Often there is some sort of loss when this card appears. Someone is trying to manipulate you to do something against your better judgment. Don't fall for it! If you're the guilty party who's attempting to mislead others, better rethink your motives.

Two of Swords

Keywords: courage, adjustment, dilemma.

Upright Position

Emotions run high. You've come to a fork in the road. It's decision time, and you can't seem to make up your mind. Your head is battling your heart. Logic takes on emotions! Keep 'em in check. Realistically, you should act now, but you probably prefer to do nothing. Don't expect fate to intervene. It is you and only you who can make a decision. Adjustments and agreements will be made shortly.

Reversed Position

You've recently made an important decision. Now the consequences of this choice are unfolding. Know that you can move forward without hesitation. There's less stress and emotional tension now. Talk openly with others about how you feel. They will understand. Have courage, and know the answers you seek are coming soon.

———————

Three of Swords

Keywords: discovery, sadness, loss.

Upright position

Sadness and tears. There's reason to cry or mourn. Perhaps you or someone close to you is going through a breakup in a romantic relationship. You may also feel bad over the loss of a friendship. Whatever type of rejection you are feeling, there are tears. But your heart will mend. Try to stay out of quarrels and arguments, as they'll only make matters worse. Sometimes this card represents surgery or dental problems.

Reversed Position

This card reversed simply means that a period of sadness is ending. In fact, you are well on your way to a wonderful recovery. Your heart may still hurt a little, but there's a lot of inner healing going on too. Know that the worst is over. You can put sorrows to rest. Expect a happier you in the days to come!

Four of Swords

Keywords: peace, balance, refuge, meditation.

Upright Position

These past few weeks have been quite stressful. You need time to recharge your batteries. A little R & R is just what the doctor ordered. Why not plan a vacation or day trip? Anything that helps you break from the same old routine will lift your spirits. This is also a fine period for meditation. Finding inner peace and listening to your higher self will supply you with all of the answers you need.

Reversed Position

Everything seems to be in a constant state of motion. You're on the go and there's no time for play. Others make heavy demands on your time. Your daily planner is filled. Be careful of overdoing things; your health could suffer. It's important to balance everything: school, friends, work, and play.

Five of Swords

Keywords: selfish, battles, ego, defeat.

Upright Position

The battle lines are drawn and someone is working against your wishes. Someone close to you is acting in a destructive, selfish manner. Egos get in the way. Keep yours in check. Examine every motive. People could be sabotaging your efforts. Watch out for sore losers and two-faced acquaintances. There's lots of gossip. You'll win any battles you fight, but they'll cost you a few friends. Choose your words carefully, as they may come back to haunt you!

Reversed Position

This is not a pleasant position for the Five of Swords to be in. It is telling you there is someone in your life that actually wants to see you fail. Trust no one. These folks could be jealous of something you do or have. Try to figure out who in your circle is two-faced. It is best not to tell him or her any secrets. This card also foretells of enemies. They'll stop at nothing to prove a point or to get their way. Unfortunately, this is not a favorable time to fight back. You simply won't win the easiest of battles, even if you are in the right.

Six of Swords

Keywords: travel, curiosity, learning.

Upright Position

You've overcome some heavy obstacles and challenges. This period of darkness is lifting slowly but surely. There is a ray of sunshine peeking through your window now. Sadness and anxiety are fading. Peace surrounds you. Good news! There's an opportunity to travel. It could be out of state or even to a foreign country. You'll certainly be excited. You may also be taking new classes or changing schools. Long lost friends may reappear in your life. There is a feeling of tranquility.

Reversed Position

The problems that have been plaguing you over the past several weeks don't seem to be getting any better. No one's coming to your rescue either! You feel trapped. It's not a favorable time to plan a trip or special event because it could get canceled. No matter how disappointing things are, you must face reality. If you don't confront challenges head on, they will subside. You can't pussy-foot around any longer.

Seven of Swords

Keywords: gossip, manipulation, theft.

Upright Position

Someone's being very sneaky. The sad part to this revelation is that this person is a trusted friend! He or she is lying or trying to cheat you. This person could be part of a new group of recent acquaintances. Sometimes the Seven of Swords represents theft, so safeguard your belongings. Also, be careful of what you say and how you say it. Words spoken could and will be held against you. Your reputation is being questioned too, and you must defend yourself.

Reversed Position

If someone has hurt or taken advantage of you, he or she will soon feel sorry! The law of karma is in effect now. Likewise, many friends will come to your aid. Don't feel sorry for yourself. You are not truly a victim unless you allow yourself to be. All will work out okay in the long run. You will get credit where credit is due. Those who try to hinder your efforts will fail.

Eight of Swords

Keywords: bad news, restricted, obstacles.

Upright Position

This card suggests you are going through a period that restricts you in some way. There are roadblocks to progress everywhere you look. Whether you recognize it or not, you have subconsciously placed these blocks on yourself. You could be your own worst enemy. Don't let old wounds lower self-esteem or hold you back from creating the wonderful and prosperous future you so desire. Be careful of little accidents or fender benders over the next few weeks.

Reversed Position

You're free! There's not a care in the world. Move forward now with plans. Your confidence is soaring as you make positive strides with new goals. A roadblock is removed. The blinders are off and you clearly see what or who was holding you back. It's full steam ahead!

Nine of Swords

Keywords: terror, frightened, fears.

Upright Position

You've drawn the nightmare card. Something is bothering you. You're not resting well. Even a deep sleep is not a peaceful one. The subconscious mind is trying to send you messages. Know that your worst fears are unfounded. Your concerns will not materialize. The difficulties you've just gone through are over. Now you're suffering the emotional aftermath. Soon you will have nothing but sweet dreams again!

Reversed Position

The terrifying nightmares are over! You may still have a few problems here and there, but things are improving. Soon, good news will replace negative thoughts and worries. You may be a little paranoid, since things have seemed difficult in your personal life, but believe me, the days are getting brighter and you are growing stronger. Don't be a prisoner of the past or allow your imagination to get the best of you. Expect nothing but good things to come to you!

Ten of Swords

Keywords: sadness, despair, lonely.

Upright Position

You've hit rock bottom and feel like giving up! There's an ending in your life. No longer can you hang on to losing propositions. You have to let go! Nothing is working out as you had hoped. Rethink your plans. There is a sense of loss and despair. A change has been forced upon you. You may react by being angry or allowing yourself to fall into a depression. Not a good idea. Prayer or mediation will help. Know that your angels are with you.

Reversed Position

Count your blessings. The worst is over. The past is behind you. A new day is dawning. There are positive changes occurring at this very moment. An old cycle of your life is ending. Darkness lifts and soon you'll greet a new day. Many will offer guidance or help. Accept their kindness. With the aid of friends, you will be able to overcome any obstacles. Things will improve now.

Page of Swords

Keywords: responsibility, promise, trust.

Upright Position

Stay clear of gossip. Don't be part of any negative talk. Someone is spreading lies to manipulate you and your friends. These lies could be about you. Malicious rumors are everywhere! There may be someone spying on you too. Unexpected problems surface with people you don't know all that well. There will be a promise made. Take it with a grain of salt, for it will be broken. For the next several weeks, be cautious about whom you choose to trust.

Reversed Position

If there's a major decision to be made, you must not take it lightly. Think things through with great care. Do not act hastily, as something is being covered up. You don't have all of the answers, so therefore confusion or a dilemma surrounds you. Refuse to sign contracts until someone you trust has time to look them over. A younger brother or sister may cause you a great deal of trouble. He or she is intentionally trying to mess with you. Someone you consider a close friend could turn on you too.

Knight of Swords

Keywords: anger, hostility, impulsiveness.

Upright Position

An unexpected blowup develops out of nowhere. There's a fierce struggle. Perhaps it's with a close friend or a significant other. Be strong now. Lead with your head rather than your heart. The Knight of Swords warns of rash, impulsive behavior in romantic relationships. Don't say things you'll later regret. If you handle things calmly and logically, there's a good chance of smoothing things over. If you don't, expect lingering disappointment with others.

Reversed Position

This is not a favorable time to start a new project or relationship. It won't work out or it will be delayed. You're not aware of it now, but someone is trying to sabotage your plans.

Without warning, you may experience a nasty breakup in a friendship. Perhaps even a romantic tie is threatened. There's a bossy, self-centered person involved in this scenario that you should steer clear of.

Queen of Swords

Keywords: grief, miscommunication, strength.

Upright Position

If there was ever a time to stand tall and voice an opinion, it's now. Let everyone know how confident you are. Go after the things you hope to accomplish. Job opportunities are plentiful, but you need to know what you really want to do. Romance takes a back seat, as time is limited. You're working overtime it seems, but what you lack in love, you'll gain in the bank book. The Queen of Swords also represents a woman close to you who is experiencing some sort of sadness or letdown. Be kind to her. Watch out for any miscommunication with females.

Reversed Position

Who is the manipulative woman around you? She is filled with negative energy and you can sense a drain on your emotions just by being around her. She wants everything "her way." If she doesn't get what she wants she can be very vengeful. It is in your best interest to stay out of her path. She cannot be trusted and is very coy. Her selfishness will be her downfall. You should try to avoid all contact with her if possible.

King of Swords

Keywords: power, ally, control, law.

Upright Position

An important decision will be made shortly. It benefits you! A strong man or father figure, perhaps a boss or teacher, is on your side. He is a great ally to have in your corner. The King of Swords also represents original thinking. Use it to help you make strides in school or on the job. You may come into contact with many professional men, such as lawyers, politicians, and entrepreneurs.

Reversed Position

You may be deceived, intimidated, or treated unfairly now. Let new acquaintances earn your trust before believing in them. Your feelings are extremely sensitive now. If you have felt betrayed, don't fight back, as you'll end up on the losing end of a proposition. It's not healthy for your self-esteem either. Don't allow yourself to be played for a fool or to be anyone's victim. Someone wants to take advantage of your kind, easygoing nature. If confronted by a bully, turn and walk away. For the next several weeks, it's in your best interest to be suspicious of anyone new you meet.

Ace of Wands

Keywords: creation, excitement, goals.

Upright Position

There's excitement in the air! You'll find yourself very enthusiastic about a new idea or goal. The energies that surround you now create the perfect type of environment for growth and success. Go after a far-fetched dream. This is a period of exciting adventures and opportunity. Enjoy the ride. If you have an idea for an invention of some sort, don't drop the ball. Run with it. This period favors all types of new creations.

Reversed Position

No matter how hard you try to get along, it seems everyone is working against you right now. Don't allow yourself to get discouraged. A commitment may be broken. You really can't depend on others, but don't abandon the sinking ship! I know you're feeling frustrated and all of your efforts seem to meet up with roadblocks. Even your enthusiasm can't seem to get you through certain barriers. Be patient. In time, the universe will work with you on building new dreams. No one will be able to stop you!

Two of Wands

Keywords: waiting, anticipation, uncertainty.

Upright Position

You have some great ideas and are chomping at the bit to make them happen. However, there are delays. You are in a holding pattern now. Use this time to examine more closely the steps you are taking to get from point A to point B. Even though this feels like a "down time," it's really an opportunity time, meant for you to reassess the path you're on. You can build a solid foundation now for future growth, as this truly is a testing period. It'll prove what you're made of.

Reversed Position

Situations you thought were under control now seem out of sorts. Nothing is moving forward. You may be working diligently on a project only to get discouraged by something or someone. You may even lose interest entirely! Don't waste a lot of precious time on something your heart isn't into in the first place. This is also a period in which you should be careful of getting into arguments with others. Everyone is at odds now. Friends you thought you could count on will not be there when you need them the most.

Three of Wands

Keywords: enthusiasm, goal-oriented, decision.

Upright Position

Any project you start now will be quite successful. Friends and family will be amazed at the talents you possess. Thoughts and ideas flow. There's a feeling of enthusiasm as you plan goals and look to the future. There could be a few job offers that drop at your feet. If one appeals to you, be sure it's something you really enjoy doing, because there are other options to consider. This card also shows a possibility for fun-filled vacations and a long-distance trip.

Reversed Position

Even though you could be facing adversity and roadblocks to progress, you are still able to make strides. You just have to slow down a bit and play a waiting game. There will be sudden and unexpected demands on your time that require undivided attention. This frustrating period gives you extra time to analyze some of your goals. Are they realistic? Could it be that you are setting your sights too high? Will it take longer to achieve your goals than originally anticipated? Are you willing to work this hard? If the answer is yes, proceed, but cut yourself some slack!

Four of Wands

Keywords: harmony, peace, happiness, attainment.

Upright Position

This card foretells of happy times, promises of peace, and a reason to throw a big party! You will achieve a long-term goal, and with it comes a feeling of added prestige (not to mention a boost in your self-confidence). Sometimes the Four of Wands indicates a birthday, an anniversary, or another happy occasion. Often it brings a residential change. Are you planning a move? Are you looking at colleges already? Need you own space? The time is ripe to make these types of changes.

Reversed Position

The Four of Wands reversed brings the same fortune as in its upright position, except success is not as grand. It's not as big of a deal. Nonetheless, you have worked hard to achieve something, and it's been a long, winding road. "Nothing worth working for comes easily," your grandfather says. You have met a number of challenges and should be quite proud of yourself. Sometimes this card promises a commitment in a love relationship. Don't get too excited. It doesn't mean marriage, only a commitment.

Five of Wands

Keywords: energy, goals, competition.

Upright Position

Ready. Set. Go! There's a challenge to meet and you're up for it. There's a new adventure right around the corner. Don't be intimidated or shy. Show everyone what you're made of. Know that you will encounter your share of rivals as you move forward. You'll have to compete against some unsavory folks if you want to win, but you'll be quite successful. If interested in someone romantically, you'll have to compete for his or her undivided attention. It's a great time to join a sports group, as you could lead your team to the victory circle.

Reversed Position

Sometimes life doesn't seem fair. People don't fight fair either. You're in a highly competitive period of life right now. Whether you're involved in sports, contests, or the game of love, understand that many of the people with whom you come into contact are opposing your efforts. People are out for themselves. Some will lie or cheat to win. This card merely warns you to take the high road, even if no one else does. Also, take better care of yourself. Get more rest.

Six of Wands

Keywords: success, recognition, honor, reward.

Upright Position

Your hard work and determination are finally paying off! If you're up for a school honor or a scholarship, you'll get it! Expect a promotion of some sort on the job, or a call back after an interview. Good news keeps on rolling in. In addition to all of the little blessings, you may find an extra big one coming your way. Say, in the form of an exciting trip or vacation. You have gained a lot of respect and admiration from your family and friends. There are lots of photographs to take as the happy times continue.

Reversed Position

This isn't a favorable time for competitions of any kind. It seems you're on the losing end of all battles. If you apply for a job, you probably won't get it. Ask someone out, and you may get snubbed. But please don't get discouraged. After all, your time is coming to bask in the sun. If you don't deal well with rejection, don't put yourself out for the next few weeks. Take time out and then proceed with plans. Life will be much easier soon.

Seven of Wands

Keywords: competition, struggle, challenge.

Upright Position

A heated argument and stiff competition lay ahead of you. There's more than one power struggle to overcome. You should not back down. I repeat, do not back down! Stand tall and defend yourself. Be firm in your convictions and with your beliefs. Giving up is not the answer. As long as you continue on your path, despite any roadblocks, victory will eventually be yours for the taking! You will learn a great deal about integrity and pride. Sometimes, this card represents a new job offer with lots of responsibility tied to it. Consider this a period in which to lay a solid foundation for future efforts.

Reversed Position

Friends may get mad at you for no apparent reason. They're not likely to confront you face to face, but instead will gossip behind your back. You need to ask them, "What's up!?" Don't get so paranoid that you lose a grip with reality, but know that words and actions can be misinterpreted. You could also get blamed for things you didn't do. Feeling picked on already? Don't be a wimp. Speak up!

Eight of Wands

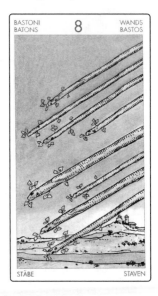

Keywords: goals, new beginnings, initiative.

Upright Position

You're on a fast track and moving with great speed! Nothing can slow you down. Your goals are reachable and in sight. Lots of folks will notice your efforts and speak highly of you. That's right! People are talking behind your back . . . in a good way! You know on a gut level that success is yours. Don't get arrogant. Be gracious and a good winner. Let everyone know how much you appreciate their support. It's as if a new and exiting path has opened up just for you. It leads to much happiness. Look for love in the most unusual places!

Reversed Position

No matter how hard you push and shove to get ahead, someone is standing in your way. There's no use crying over it. Just find a different route to take. Don't get discouraged, but know you must change your plans a bit in order to find true success. Your parents and teachers may not be as understanding as they have been in the past with your excuses and dilemmas. You feel as if everyone is arguing with you. Nobody understands! This time will pass. Just make sure you don't say or do anything you may regret later on.

Nine of Wands

Keywords: defense, challenge.

Upright Position

There is a challenge that must be met. There's no way around it. Stand tall and strong in your convictions. Tackle any problems as they come up. Putting them off will only make things worse. You may feel as if you are failing, but you won't fail. Fight for what you believe in. Taking care of business is the main theme here. You're on the defensive, but you'll win the case. If you back down, more conflicts will arise.

Reversed Position

Better take care of yourself. Don't let your immune system run down or you'll be stuck indoors with a nasty cold for a while. Looking at the Nine of Wands from another standpoint, there could be disappointment in someone or something you once strongly believed in. This issue is not worth fighting for. Don't shed any more tears. It's best to let go of false hopes. You're only looking at a situation from a standpoint of what could be, not what truly is. So take off your rose-colored glasses and see people and situations in a true light. Anything you're fighting for is not worth the effort. Let it go.

Ten of Wands

Keywords: tired, drained, responsibility.

Upright Position

It appears you have taken on too many responsibilities. There's a flurry of activity as school or work projects appear to be overwhelming. Don't worry. This period will pass and soon you will have a lot of free time to do things you really enjoy. You see, the Ten of Wands teaches you about being responsible for your actions, about commitment and promises. There will be a reward for all of your hard work and efforts. Don't get discouraged. Sweet success will soon be yours!

Reversed Position

Consider this a positive and powerful position for the Ten of Wands. All of your hard work is paying off and there is a light at the end of the tunnel. If there's been stress and anxiety in your life, it is now fading away. Soon, you'll be able to kick back with friends and enjoy yourself more than ever. There's a satisfaction in knowing you've completed a task or project. I may add, you did a very good job!

Page of Wands

Keywords: love, attraction, competition.

Upright Position

Are you longing for a bit of romance in your life? You could find it right around the corner. A close friend may actually be your secret admirer. Imagine that! You're looking and feeling fine. Everyone notices your natural glow and feels attracted to you. If you've been putting off an exercise program, now is the time to start it because you'll have more determination to stick to a plan than ever before. This card also suggests great news coming via e-mail or the telephone. Perhaps a call for a new job? Maybe a hot date? Make sure you're easy to get ahold of these days. If you go out, leave your answering machine on!

Reversed Position

There's unexpected, disturbing news coming. It could mean a breakup in a committed relationship. Maybe you didn't make the cut on the team or perhaps you will be turned down for a job promotion. Don't let this bother you. Anything that happens now happens for a reason. Perhaps you should look at alternatives and other options you didn't consider before. Know that things don't stay the same forever. This is a time to stay away from gossip. Also, don't share secrets.

Knight of Wands

Keywords: adventure, wisdom, travel.

Upright Position

New faces and new places dominate the picture now. Expect some interesting changes to occur too! One may be moving, starting a new school, or enjoying a new hobby. Someone special may also come into your life at this time. He or she offers wisdom and guidance and will be a great benefit to you in some way. Perhaps this person is a teacher or a new coach. Pay close attention to what he or she has to tell you. This card also suggests that a fun-filled trip will be planned shortly. Save some money to shop!

Reversed Position

Someone around you now cannot be trusted. He or she appears to be very charming, friendly, and outgoing but is actually quite manipulative. Also, be aware of a problem with your schoolwork. Double check everything. It's not easy to keep your grades up for some reason. It's easy to fall behind in a particular class. If you're seeing someone exclusively, watch out for communication problems. Both of you need to be honest with one another. If not, there will be a major blowup in the next week or two.

Queen of Wands

Keywords: business-sense, strong, fair, loyal.

Upright Position

This Queen of Wands represents a business-minded woman. She is career-oriented. This card also suggests that you are acting in a mature, professional manner. Someone close to you, likely a female, is in your corner. She is trustworthy and loyal. Any involvement you have with strong women will be to your benefit. If you are employed and working under a female supervisor, ask her for a raise. She is feeling quite generous at this time! Spend more time with your mom too. You'll enjoy her company and create some lasting memories together. There's a helpful, kind, and loyal female friend in your life, and she has your best interests at heart.

Reversed Position

There's a bossy, rude woman who insists on getting her way. She is a thorn in everyone's side, and especially yours! You have to deal with her. There's no way to avoid this gal. But be careful that she doesn't try to blackmail or block your efforts. This Queen also warns you to mind your own business. It's best to stay out of a friend's problem now because you may get the blame for anything that goes wrong. Choose your words carefully. Gossip is everywhere!

King of Wands

Keywords: experience, help, honesty, ally.

Upright Position

Expect a strong ally in your corner soon. He's likely to be an older man who is respected and admired by many. He could bring financial help or offer you a job. He has your best interest at heart and will take you under his wing. Allow him to teach you new things. There is much to learn, and this King wants to graciously help. This card foretells of much recognition and success if you're willing to work hard toward a chosen goal. Most of your close relationships run smoothly, and you feel good about those around you. Some new acquaintances will enter your life now, and they will be a great benefit too.

Reversed Position

Be aware of deceptive people around you, especially men who have strong, overbearing personalities. Some will seem arrogant and downright rude. If you encounter a man you immediately dislike or are intimidated by, let this be a warning: Stay away from him; he can only mean trouble. He lies and cheats to get his way and plans to make you a part of his game. Nothing stands in his way of personal gain. He is ruthless and a con artist. Also, this card is warning you that you could be taken advantage of by others, perhaps within the next few days or weeks. Don't get tricked by people who make things out to be more spectacular than they really are. Don't bow to any type of peer pressure either.

Afterword

YOU'VE JUST COMPLETED one part of your journey. Now, put what you've learned to the test and start reading for your friends and family. Let your conscience be your guide. Allow your intuition to grow and flourish. Remember, we are all blessed with spiritual gifts, and it's our responsibility to use these gifts to help others. The more readings you do, the more your intuition will grow. One thing you should keep in mind, however, is that not everyone will share the same viewpoint as you do about using these gifts. Only share the tarot with people who appreciate and acknowledge that it is a wonderful tool. Also, make sure you don't allow the tarot to become the last word in everything you say or do. It is only meant to be a helpful guide.

Ultimately, you must make up your own mind and follow your conscience when it comes to making decisions. The tarot is designed to help you, but not to be the final word or authority. You are the only one responsible for your thoughts and actions. Oftentimes a reading will confirm what you've already been feeling. It's a wonderful way to explore the depths of your intuitive side.

Enjoy your journey!